THE ORTHODOX CHURCH

THE ORTHODOX CHURCH

SERGIUS BULGAKOV
1871-1944

with a foreword

by

THOMAS HOPKO

Translation revised by
Lydia Kesich

St. Vladimir's Seminary Press
Crestwood, New York 10707
1988

Originally published in Russian
Translated into English and first
published in 1935 by Centenary Press, London

Library of Congress Cataloging in Publication Data

Bulgakov, Sergeï Nikolaevich, 1871-1944.
  [Pravoslavie. English]
  The Orthodox Church / Sergius Bulgakov ; with a foreword by Thomas
  Hopko ; translation revised by Lydia Kesich.
      p. cm.
  Translation of: Pravoslavie.
  ISBN 0-88141-051-9 : $8.95
  1. Orthodox Eastern Church--Doctrines. I. Title.
BX320.2.B813   1988
281.9--dc19   88-1851
                                                           CIP

THE ORTHODOX CHURCH

This revised translation © 1988

by

ST. VLADIMIR'S
SEMINARY PRESS

ISBN 0-88141-051-9

PRINTED IN THE UNITED STATES OF AMERICA
by
J & J Printing, Inc.
Syracuse, New York

Contents

Foreword

More than fifty years have passed since Father Sergius Bulgakov wrote the book which was immediately translated into English in an abridged form as THE ORTHODOX CHURCH, and is now being made available in this revised edition. Although gifted with prophetic insight, the author could hardly have forseen the radical changes in the Christian world, and in the world generally, which have occurred since his book was originally published.

Sergius Bulgakov's personal story, learned from his autobiographical writings (key parts of which are translated into English[1]) is rather well known; while his complicated theology remains generally unstudied even by students of Orthodox theology and Russian religious thought. The man's life and experience, however, with his basic insights and intuitions, are undoubtedly of greater significance for us today than the fine points of his thinking, which, according to his own testimony, are probative and tentative, in need of careful analysis within the Christian community.

Bulgakov's Life

Bulgakov was born in Russia in 1871 into the family of an Orthodox priest. He lost his childhood faith, as did so many others of the clerical caste, as a teen-age seminarian whose questions could

---

[1]See Sergius Bulgakov, *A Bulgakov Anthology,* edited by James Pain and Nicholas Zernov, with an introduction by James Pain and a memoir by Lev Zander *(Philadelphia: The Westminister Press, 1976.)* Nicholas O. Lossky, *History of Russian Philosophy* (New York: International Universities Press, 1951) pp. 192-232. V.V. Zenkovsky, *A History of Russian Philosophy,* Volume Two (New York: Columbia University Press, 1953) pp. 890-916. Nicholas Zernov, *The Russian Religious Renaissance of the Twentieth Century* (London: Darton, Longman & Todd, 1963.)

not be answered by the text-book theology of the day; whose emotions could not endure the endless church services whose inner truth and beauty remained concealed under the formality of their performance; and whose sense of freedom and justice could not accept the political and social conditions of imperial Russia on the brink of revolution. He remained an atheist, and an enthusiastic Marxist, until his mind and heart revolted against the results of his economic and legal studies. In his thirtieth year, following a number of religious experiences mediated through nature and art which he interpreted in the light of German philosophical idealism and the mystical intuitions of Solovyov and Dostoevsky, he returned to the church of his childhood.

On the feast of the Holy Spirit in 1918, in the church of the Holy Spirit at the Danilov Monastery in Moscow (now returned to the Russian Church and restored to its former magnificence) Sergius Bulgakov yielded to his ''levite blood'' and was ordained an Orthodox priest. He had been ordained deacon on the previous day of Pentecost. Many of his friends, including those who had made the same journey ''from Marxism to idealism'' and into the Church, were present to witness the event: Father Pavel Florensky, Nikolai Berdyaev, Petr Struve, Vyacheslav Ivanov, Prince Evgenii Trubetskoy and others. The experience of ordination, Bulgakov wrote, was ''like going through fire, scorching, cleansing and regenerating''; a gift of indescribable joy about which he could only ''keep silent.''[2] His ministry, however, was not to be accomplished in his native land. After a few years of service in the Crimea where he had been forced by the events of the revolution to remain when visiting his family, he was exiled from Russia forever in 1923.

Father Bulgakov settled first in Prague where he taught at the Russian Law Institute and was a leading participant in the Russian Student Christian Movement. By 1925 he was in Paris assisting in the establishment of St. Sergius Orthodox Theological Institute, the Russian emigre school which he served as dean until his death in

---

[2]Pain and Zernov (1976) p.8

1944. He lived at the institute with his wife and children, two sons and a daughter. A third son had died at the age of three in Russia in 1909, an event which had a profound effect on Bulgakov's journey.

Father Bulgakov was the professor of dogmatic theology at St. Sergius, and served as priest in the seminary chapel. He exercised an extensive pastoral ministry as counselor and confessor in addition to his professorial duties. He was a pioneer in ecumenical activities as one of the original founders of the Fellowship of St. Alban and St. Sergius and a participant in the Faith and Order movement, representing Orthodoxy at the conferences in Lausanne, Oxford and Edinburgh. He visited the United States and Canada in 1934 at the invitation of the Episcopal Church. While Bulgakov's economic and philosophical works, including his first sophiological reflections, THE UNFADING LIGHT, were mostly written before his exile, his famous theological works were all produced in Paris.

In 1939 Father Bulgakov underwent surgery for throat cancer which left him almost completely unable to speak. He continued to conduct his classes, making comments and answering questions while another read his lecture notes. He also continued to celebrate the eucharist on certain weekday mornings, an event which attracted numbers of his disciples to the seminary chapel. He served his last divine liturgy on the day of his priestly ordination, the feast of the Holy Spirit, in 1944. He had a cerebral stroke that evening from which he never recovered. He died forty days later on the twelfth of July.

Bulgakov's Works

THE ORTHODOX CHURCH is the best known of Father Bulgakov's works. Published in English in 1935, and subsequently in French and other languages, it was intended to be a general introduction to Eastern Orthodoxy for Western Christians. It has superbly served this purpose, and will continue to do so with this present edition, enlightening not only the non-Orthodox, but also the new Orthodox who have joined the Church, and the countless others who have been raised in the Faith but remain ignorant of its teachings.

None of Bulgakov's theological works are translated into English:—the shorter works on the apostles (PETER AND JOHN, 1926), the Virgin Mary (THE UNCONSUMED BUSH, 1927), John the Baptist (THE FRIEND OF THE BRIDEGROOM, 1928), the angels (JACOB'S LADDER, 1929), and the holy icons (ICONS AND THEIR VENERATION, 1931); the major trilogy on Christ (THE LAMB OF GOD, 1933), the Holy Spirit (The COMFORTER, 1936), and the Church (THE BRIDE OF THE LAMB, 1945); and his final work on the book of Revelation (THE JOHANNINE APOCALYSPE, 1948). THE ORTHODOX CHURCH, together with the short summary of his ''sophiology'' entitled THE WISDOM OF GOD (London, 1937), are virtually the sole sources of Bulgakov's thought available to English-speaking readers.[3]

Bulgakov's Sophiology

THE ORTHODOX CHURCH is not a controversial book, at least by Bulgakovian standards. There are questionable things in it, especially in view of the changes which have occurred since its original appearance, particularly in Roman Catholicism and Anglicanism. Its debatable points, however, have virtually nothing to do with the author's ''sophiology'' which led in his lifetime, and until today, to accusations of ''heresy.''

Whatever he was, Father Sergius Bulgakov was not a heretic. Like others before him, including saints such as Augustine of Hippo (with whom Father Bulgakov invites intriguing comparison) and Gregory of Nyssa, Father Bulgakov was a bold and brilliant thinker

---

[3]In addition to *A Bulgakov Anthology* cited above, selections of Bulgakov's writings in English may be found in Alexander Schmemann, *Ultimate Questions: An Anthology of Russian Thought* (Crestwood, N.Y.: SVS Press, 1965.) Access to his theological ideas are also available in English in doctoral dissertations such as that of Charles Graves, *The Holy Spirit in the Theology of Sergius Bulgakov,* (printed privately at the WCC, Geneva, Switzerland, 1973).

whom many judge to be mistaken in certain of his ideas and faulty in certain of his conceptualizations. His errors, most critics say, come from philosophical influences outside the Christian tradition, coupled with the fervent desire to make the Church's vision and experience available to people who were unable, and perhaps unwilling, to accept customary presentations of the Faith in a time of change, confusion and chaos of apocalyptic proportions.

Father Bulgakov never doubted the truth of Orthodoxy. He created no formal schisms or divisions in the Church. He was never deprived of his chair of dogmatic theology or his deanship at St. Sergius. He was never suspended from the priesthood or removed from the Church's communion. When his teachings were formally questioned by the Moscow Patriarchate, his apology was accepted by his archbishop, Metropolitan Eulogius, who eulogized him at his funeral as "a teacher of the Church in the purest and most lofty sense (who was) enlightened by the Holy Spirit, the Spirit of Wisdom, the Spirit of Understanding, the Comforter to whom (he) dedicated (his) scholarly work." Bulgakov commended his work to the Church for judgment; obviously believing that he would be justified in his doctrines, yet fully prepared to have his vision tested by the common mind of the faithful.

Such times as those in which Bulgakov lived—the end of old regimes in many nations, including his own; unprecedented scientific, social, economic and political revolution; radical ecclesiastical reform; massive intellectual and artistic ferment; wholesale displacement and exile; two great world wars; holocausts, genocides, exterminations, Gulags—cannot fail to incite courageous Christians to action while inviting the fainthearted to take refuge in formalistic repetitions of customary teachings. Such times also inevitably tempt the bold to indiscretion, firing the enthusiasm of the Lord's "hot" disciples who fear being spewn from his mouth for their indifferences and cowardice in the face of evil and apostasy. (See Rev. 3:16).

Father Bulgakov was certainly a "hot" man: bold, enthusiastic, prophetic, apocalyptic. It seems sure that he was somewhat seduced by his own talents and inventiveness, his daring and enthusiasm, and his hard-won certitude that Christ and the Church are the sole source of truth, beauty and life for a world gone mad in its worship of Man. He was certainly convinced that a main reason for the disasters which he witnessed was the truly heretical Christian teaching which split the Creator from His good creation, and surrendered the world—which God so loved that He sent His Son for its salvation—into the hands of the godless.

Father Bulgakov could not abide a church caught up in a cultic ecclesiasticism. And he could not endure a world surrendered to ungodly secularism. His "sophiology" was his response to this frustration. However mistaken his teachings, however in need of critique and correction, they are certainly conceived in passion, born in agony, fueled by polemics, fired by apologetics, tempted by creative brilliance, and maintained by their author's adamant refusal, surely not free from stubborness and pride, to repeat the safe sentences of the insecure who are hardly without a stubborn pride of their own.

The Orthodox Church

THE ORTHODOX CHURCH contains little "sophiology." There are strains of it in passing, but nothing calling for extensive commentary. The Trinitarian reflections in the book's early pages reflect it, as do the author's eschatological and apocalyptic musings in the later chapters, with his obvious interest in promoting a type of Christian universalism. The mistake here, which is made by others, but is always particularly noted in Bulgakov's case, is to equate a doctrine of the unending torment of the wicked with a doctrine of God's just need to punish sinners in conflict with His mercy and love. Bulgakov attributes this doctrine to negative Western influences on Orthodoxy, a charge found often in his writings to which, ironically, he himself was hardly immune.

The classical patristic explanation about "everlasting hell," especially that of the mystical writers, seems to disagree with what

Father Bulgakov both opposes and defends. It rather holds that it is precisely the presence of God's mercy and love which cause the torment of the wicked. God does not punish; he forgives. Sinful creatures may refuse His forgiveness. This refusal (which may be unending since human free choice can never be destroyed) makes hell to be hell. In a word, God has mercy on all, whether all like it or not. If we like it, it is paradise; if we do not, it is hell. Every knee will bend before the Lord. Everything will be subject to Him. God in Christ will indeed be "all and in all," with boundless mercy and unconditional pardon. But not all will rejoice in God's gift of forgiveness, and that choice will be their judgment, the self-inflicted source of their sorrow and pain.

The weakest parts of Bulgakov's book are the chapters on the sacraments and church services. These, more than the slightly veiled "sophiologies" which appear from time to time, reveal the author's inability to be free from the Western influences on Orthodox thought and life which he himself so often laments. Readers trained in Orthodox theology in the last quarter century will find these pages disappointing, and perhaps even shocking, coming from a theologian of Bulgakov's stature and reputation. And the neophyte to Orthodoxy must surely be directed to the works of others such as Father Alexander Schmemann for a presentation of Orthodox liturgy more in keeping with the Church's own witness in her sacramental rites and the apostolic and patristic commentaries which explain them.[4]

Bulgakov's chapter on the Bible and Tradition remains a masterful exposition of the subject. Except for his remarks about Roman Catholic and Anglican biblical studies which no longer apply, his classically Orthodox presentation in many ways anticipates the con-

[4]See the SVS Press publications by Alexander Schmemann, *Introduction to Liturgical Theology* (1966, 1986), *For the Life of the World: Sacraments and Orthodoxy* (1963, 1973), *Of Water and the Spirit* (1974), *Great Lent* (1969), *The Eucharist* (1988). Also A. Schmemann, *Liturgy and Life: Christian Development through Liturgical Experience* (New York: Department of Religious Education, Orthodox Church in America, 1974).

clusions of the Fourth WCC Faith and Order Conference which met on this theme in 1963 in Montreal.

The longest and still most important chapter in THE OR-THODOX CHURCH is the one on the hierarchy. It is a meditation on the nature, structure and task of the Christian Church. The subject is that which has been most radically confronted and changed in Christian life and teaching since the book was written, especially since the Second Vatican Council of the Roman Catholic Church and the achievements of the ecumenical movement. Despite the many changes which have taken place, however, with the many fruits of modern biblical, liturgical, historial and patristic studies which have served to bring them about, the nature of the Church and her ministry still remain the most controverted issues facing Christians today. They continue to cause the greatest disagreement and difficulty within ecclesial communions (including the Orthodox Church), as well as between them.

Hierarchal and Conciliar

There never was a time since Pentecost when the one, holy, catholic, and apostolic Church of Christ—the church which is His body, the fullness of Him who fills all in all (Eph 1:23); the pillar and bulwark of the truth (1 Tim 3:15) (to invoke two of Bulgakov's favorite scriptual passages)—has failed to exist. This Church, according to Father Bulgakov, is the Orthodox Church. It is a conciliar, sobornal body which is also hierarchal, in imitation of the Holy Trinity. It is a charismatic, prophetic body possessing in perfect freedom, through the unity of all its members, both clerical and lay, the full unity of faith and life guaranteed to it by God through Christ and the Holy Spirit.

To believe, understand and live the experience of the Church is to participate in the being and life of God and His kingdom. This is what the Church brings to the fallen world. It is the reason for her existence. Schisms and heresies inevitably come, that the genuine may be recognized. (1 Cor 11:11). But they do not effect the

Church's God-given being and mission, however sinful her earthly members may be.

The task of the hierarchy is to guarantee and protect the Church's unity, identity, integrity, solidarity and continuity in space and time. It can do this only in communion with, and not over or apart from, the whole body of the faithful. Any of the Church's hierarchs may err. Even great numbers of them gathered in solemn assembly may do so, and have. No bishop or council is infallible in itself. Christ's Church, however, is infallible, and manifests herself as such in history through the succession of churches whose bishops and people remain faithful to her apostolic doctrine and ministry.

These ecclesiological doctrines of Orthodoxy cannot be repeated too frequently or forcefully. We Orthodox must face them squarely since we cannot deny that our actual ecclesial structures, attitudes and actions are in clear contradiction with our theological vision. And the non-Orthodox must face them as well, as the bitter controversies concerning authority, jurisdiction, magisterium, ordination and ministry in all their churches bear sad and eloquent testimony.

Church and World

Father Bulgakov's vision of the Church and the world, especially his ideas presented in THE ORTHODOX CHURCH in his brief chapters on ethics, economics, social and political life, and eschatology—which naturally flow from his general theological vision—remain strikingly relevant. They may even be more significant today than when they were originally written. The secularization of European and American life; issues of the relation of religion to public life and its involvement in it; the emergence of the various liberation movements and theologies; the Christian engagement with Marxism; the meeting of the various "world religions"; the appearance of numberless ethical issues, with their legal ramifications, emerging from technological developments; the cosmological issues raised by everchanging and conflicting scientific world-views...all seem to have been foreseen by Father Bulgakov, and enthusiastically greeted as opportunities for positive Christian contribution when approached from the perspective and experience of Orthodoxy.

For all the tragedies which he endured—personal, national and ecclesiastical—Father Bulgakov remained a Christian optimist to the end. He never underestimated the power of evil, but firmly believed that Jesus Christ is more powerful. He never doubted that God's world belongs to the Lamb, and to those washed in his blood; and that the Church—the Orthodox Church—is his beloved Bride. For Father Bulgakov the children of light are stronger than the children of darkness, and in the end it is they who conquer.

"Come, Lord Jesus!" was the cry not only of Bulgakov's lips, but of his life. For this alone his mistakes may be pardoned and his transgressions, voluntary and involuntary, forgiven. Those who are serious in their seekings, whatever their theological and spiritual convictions, are obligated at some point to come to terms with Father Sergius Bulgakov. The results for the courageous cannot fail to be enlightening and inspiring; perhaps not in the ways that the Russian thinker imagined, but in ways known to the Master he served.

— Thomas Hopko
St. Vladimir's Seminary

CHAPTER 1

THE CHURCH

Orthodoxy is the Church of Christ on earth. The Church of Christ is not an institution; it is a new life with Christ and in Christ, guided by the Holy Spirit. Christ, the Son of God, came to earth, was made man, uniting His divine life with that of humanity. This divine-human life He gave to His brethren, who believe on His name. Although He died and rose again and ascended into heaven, He was not separated from His humanity, but remains in it. The light of the resurrection of Christ lights the Church, and the joy of resurrection, of the triumph over death, fills it. The risen Lord lives with us and our life in the Church is a mysterious life in Christ. "Christians" bear that name precisely because they belong to Christ, they live in Christ, and Christ lives in them. The Incarnation is not only an idea or a doctrine; it is above all an event which happened once in time but which possesses all the power of eternity, and this perpetual incarnation, a perfect, indissoluble union, yet without confusion, of the two natures — divine and human — makes the Church. Since the Lord did not merely approach humanity but became one with it, Himself becoming man, the Church is the Body of Christ, as a unity of life with Him, a life subordinate to Him and under His authority. The same idea is expressed when the Church is called the Bride of Christ or of the Word; the relations between bride and bridegroom, taken in their everlasting fullness, consist of a perfect unity of life, a unity which preserves the reality of their difference: it is a union of two in one, which is not dissolved by duality nor absorbed by unity. The Church, although it is the Body of Christ, is not the Christ — the God-Man — because it is only His humanity; but it is life in Christ, and with Christ, the life of Christ in us; "it is no longer I who live, but Christ Who lives in me" (Gal. 2:20). But Christ is not only a Divine Person. Since His own life is inseparable from that of the Holy Trinity, His life is con-

1

substantial with that of the Father and the Holy Spirit. Thus it is that, although a life in Christ, the Church is also a life in the Holy Trinity. The body of Christ lives in Christ, and by that very fact in the Holy Trinity. Christ is the Son. In Him we learn to know the Father, we are adopted by God, to Whom we cry "Our Father."

The love of God, the love of the Father for the Son and that of the Son for the Father, is not a simple quality or relation; it possesses itself a personal life, it is hypostatic. The love of God is the Holy Spirit, which proceeds from the Father to the Son, abiding upon Him. The Son exists for the Father only in the Holy Spirit which rests on Him, as the Father manifests his love for the Son by the Holy Spirit, which is the unity of life of Father and Son. And the Spirit itself, being the love of two persons, in keeping with the very nature of love lives, so to speak, in Its personal existence outside Itself in the Father and the Son. This is love: living, It dies, and dying, It lives. In the moment when It seems to efface itself, It exercises the greatest force. This is the place of the Holy Spirit in the Holy Trinity.

The Church, in her quality of Body of Christ, which lives with the life of Christ, is by that fact the domain where the Holy Spirit lives and works. More: the Church is life by the Holy Spirit, because it is the Body of Christ. This is why the Church may be considered life in the Holy Spirit, or the life of the Holy Spirit in humanity.

The essence of this doctrine is revealed in its historical manifestation. The Church is the work of the Incarnation of Christ, it is the Incarnation itself. God takes unto Himself human nature, and human nature assumes divinity: it is the deification of human nature, result of the union of the two natures in Christ. But at the same time the work of assimilating humanity into the Body of Christ is not accomplished by virtue of the Incarnation alone, or even by the Resurrection alone. "It is to your advantage that I go away [to my Father]" (John 16:7). That work required the sending of the Holy Spirit, Pentecost, which was the fulfillment of the Church. The Holy Spirit, in the form of tongues of fire, descended upon the world and rested on the Apostles. The unity of these, the unity of the twelve presided over by the Blessed Virgin, represents the whole of mankind. The tongues of fire remained in the world and formed the treasure of the gifts of the Holy Spirit which reside in the Church. This gift of the Holy Spirit was conferred in the primitive Church by the Apostles after baptism; now the corresponding gift, the "seal of the gift of the Holy Spirit," is accorded in the sacrament of chrismation.

The Church, then, is the Body of Christ. Through the Church we participate in the divine life of the Holy Trinity, it is life in the Holy Spirit by which we become children of the Father and which cries in our souls: "Abba, Father," and which reveals to us the Christ living in us. That is why, before attempting any definition of the Church as manifested in history, we ought to understand the Church as a sort of divine fixed quantity living in itself and comparable only with itself, as the will of God manifesting itself in the world.

The Church exists, it is "given" in a certain sense, independently of its historic origin; it took form because it already existed in the divine, superhuman plan. It exists in us, not as an institution or a society, but first of all as a spiritual certainty, a special experience, a new life. The preaching of primitive Christianity is the joyous and triumphant announcement of that new life. The life is indefinable, but it can be described and it can be lived.

There can thus be no satisfactory and complete definition of the Church. "Come and see"—one recognizes the Church only by experience, by grace, by participation in its life. This is why before making any formal definition, the Church must be conceived in its mystical being, underlying all definitions, but larger than them all. The Church, in its essence as a divine-human unity, belongs to the realm of the divine. It is from God, but it exists in the world, in human history. However, if the Church is considered only in its historic development and if it is conceived only as a society on this earth, its original nature is not understood, that quality of expressing the eternal in the temporal, of showing the uncreated in the created.

The essence of the Church is the divine life, revealing itself in the life of the creature; it is the deification of the creature by the power of the Incarnation and of Pentecost. That life is a supreme reality, it is evident and certain for all those who participate in it. Nevertheless, it is a spiritual life, hidden in the "secret man," in the "inner chamber" of his heart; in this sense it is a mystery and a sacrament. It is above nature — in other words, it exists apart from the world; still it is included within the life of the world. These two attributes are equally characteristic. From the viewpoint of the former, we say the Church is "invisible," different from all that is visible in the world, from all that is the object of perception among the things of the world. One might say that it does not exist in this world, and, judging by experience (in Kant's use of the term), we encounter no "phenomenon" which corresponds to the Church; the hypothesis of the Church is as superfluous for experimental cosmology as the hypothesis of God for the cosmology of Laplace. Thus it is correct to speak, if not of a Church invisible, at least of the invisible in the Church. Nevertheless, this invisible is not unknown, for, beyond the scope of the senses, man possesses "spiritual vision," by means of which he sees, he conceives, he knows. This vision is faith, which in the words of the Apostle, is "the conviction of things not seen" (Heb. 11:1); it lifts us on wings to the spiritual realm, it makes us citizens of the heavenly world. The life of the Church is the life of faith, by means of which the things of this world become transparent. And, naturally, these spiritual eyes can see the Church "invisible." If the Church were really invisible, completely imperceptible, that would mean simply that there were no Church, for the Church cannot exist solely in itself apart from mankind. It is not altogether included in human experience, for the life of the Church is divine and inexhaustible, but a certain quality of that life, a certain experience of the life in the Church, is given to everyone who approaches it. In this sense everything in the Church is invisible and mysterious, it all surpasses the limits of the visible world; but still the invisible may become visible, and the fact that we may see the invisible is the very condition of the existence of the Church.

Thus the Church in its very being is an object of faith; it is known by faith: ''I believe in one holy Catholic and Apostolic Church.'' The Church is perceived by faith, not only as a quality or an experience, but also quantitatively: as an all-embracing unity, as a life unique and integral, as universality, after the pattern of the oneness of the three Persons of the Holy Trinity. Only the infinite subdivision of the human species is accessible to our sight; we see how each individual leads a life egotistical and isolated. The children of the same Adam, although they are social creatures, altogether dependent on their brothers, do not perceive their essential unity, but this unity manifests itself in love and by love, and it exists by virtue of participation in the one divine life of the Church. ''Let us love one another that in the same spirit we may confess'' proclaims the Church during the liturgy. That unity of the Church reveals itself to the eyes of love not at all as an exterior union — after the fashion of those we meet in every human society — but as the mysterious, original source of life. Humanity is one in Christ, men are branches of one vine, members of one body. The life of each man enlarges itself infinitely into the life of others, the ''communio sanctorum,'' and each man in the Church lives the life of all men in the Church; each man is humanity: (''homo sum et nihil humanum a me alienum esse puto''). He belongs not only to that part of humanity which, living on earth at the moment, stands before God in prayer and labor, for the present generation is only a page in the book of life. In God and His Church, there is no difference between living and dead, and all are one in the love of the Father. Even the generations yet to be born are part of this one divine humanity.

But the Church universal is not limited to humanity alone; the whole company of the angels is equally a part of it. The very existence of the world of angels is inaccessible to human sight; it can be affirmed only by spiritual experience and perceived only by the eyes of faith. And thus our union in the Church becomes even larger through the Son of God, in that He has reunited things earth-

ly and things heavenly, has destroyed the wall of partition between
the world of angels and the world of men. Then to all humanity and
to the assembly of angels is added all nature, the whole of creation.
It is entrusted to the guardianship of angels and given to man that
he may rule over it; it shares the destiny of man. ''The whole creation has been groaning in travail together'' (Rom. 8:22-23), to be
transfigured in a ''new creation,'' simultaneous with our resurrection. In the Church man thus becomes a universal being; his life in
God unites him to the life of all creation by the bonds of cosmic
love. Such are the boundaries of the Church. And that Church,
which unites not only the living but the dead, the hierarchies of
angels and all creation, that Church is invisible, but not unknown.
The life of the Church is before the beginning of the world of man
and is lost in eternity.

It may be said that the Church was the preeternal purpose and the
foundation of creation; in this sense it was created before all things,
and for it the world was made. The Lord God created man in His
image, and thus made possible the penetration of man by the spirit
of the Church and the Incarnation of God, for God could take upon
Himself only the nature of a being who corresponded to Him and
who in itself contained His image. In the integral unity of humanity
there is already present the germ of the unity of the Church in the
image of the Holy Trinity. Thus it is difficult to point to a time
when the Church did not exist in humanity, at least in the state of
previous design. According to the doctrine of the Fathers, a primordial Church already existed in Paradise before the fall, when the
Lord went to speak with man and put Himself into relation with
him. After the fall, in the first words about the ''seed of the
woman'' the Lord laid the foundation of what may be termed the
Church of the old covenant, the Church wherein man learned to
commune with God. And even in the darkness of paganism, in the
natural seeking of the human soul for its God, there existed a
''pagan sterile church'' as some of the songs of the Church call it.
Certainly the Church attained the fullness of its existence only with
the Incarnation, and in this sense the Church was founded by Our

Lord Jesus Christ and realized at Pentecost. On this event, the foundation of the Church was laid, but its fullness is not yet attained. It is still the Church militant, and it must become the Church triumphant, where "God shall be all in all."

It is impossible, then, to define the limits of the Church in space, in time, or in power of action, and in this sense the Church, although not invisible, is not completely comprehensible; nevertheless that does not make the Church invisible in the sense that it does not exist on earth under a form accessible to experience, or even in the sense that it is transcendent only, which would in reality mean its non-existence. No, although we do not comprehend its whole meaning, the Church is visible on the earth, it is quite accessible to our experience, it has its limits in time and space. The life invisible of the Church, the life of faith, is indissolubly connected with the concrete forms of earthly life. "The invisible" exists in the visible, is included in it; together they form a symbol. The word "symbol" denotes a thing which belongs to this world, which is closely allied to it, but which has nevertheless a content in existence before all ages. It is the unity of the transcendent and the immanent, a bridge between heaven and earth, a unity of God and man, the God and the creature. In this sense the life of the Church is symbolic; it is a mysterious life, hidden under visible signs. The contrast between "the Church invisible" and the visible human society, a contrast arising because of the interior Church, but foreign to it, that contradistinction destroys the symbol; it invalidates the Church itself, as a union of the divine life and the life of the creature transcending the Church in the realm of the "noumenal," and thus lessening the value of the "phenomenal."

But if the Church as life is contained in the earthly Church, then this earthly Church, like all reality here below, has its limits in time and space. Being not only a society, not comprehended in or limited by that concept, still it exists exactly as a society, which has its own characteristics, its laws and limits. It is for us and in us, in our temporal existence. The Church has a history, just as everything that exists in the world lives in history. Thus the existence, external, unmoved, divine, of the Church appears in the life of this age as an historic manifestation, has its beginning in history. The Church was founded by Our Lord Jesus Christ; He has ordained that the profession of faith Peter, spoken in the name of all the Apostles, should be the cornerstone of His Church. After the resurrection He sent the Apostles to preach His Church; it is from the descent of the Holy Spirit on the Apostles that the Church of the New Covenant dates its existence—at that time there rang from the mouth of Peter the first apostolic appeal inviting entrance into the Church: "Repent, and be baptized everyone of you in the name of Jesus Christ..., and you shall receive the gift of the Holy Spirit" (Acts 2:38); "And there were added that day about three thousand souls" (Acts 2:41). Thus was laid the foundation of the Church of the New Covenant.

CHAPTER 2

THE CHURCH AS TRADITION
Holy Scripture and Holy Tradition

Not the whole of the human race belongs to the Church, only the elect. And not all Christians belong in the fullest sense, to the Church — only Orthodox. Both these facts give rise to problems for the searching reason and for religious faith. Both problems have exhausted the theologians. How can it be, if Christ took upon Himself a whole humanity, that the body of the Church, His Church, comprehends externally only that part of humanity which is in the Church? And how is it that of that section of humanity called to the love of Christ by baptism, only a portion live the true life of the Church, elect from among the elect? The Lord has given us no understanding of the first problem, and only a partial comprehension of the second, which we shall consider later. The salvation of mankind through entrance into the Church is not a mechanical process, independent of the will of man, but it presupposes the voluntary acceptance or rejection of Christ (Mark 16:16). Thus by faith one enters the Church; by lack of faith one leaves it. The Church, as an earthly society, is first of all a unity of faith, of the true faith preached to the world by the Apostles after the descent of the Holy Spirit. Since this faith must be expressed in words, confession and, preaching, the Church appears as a society joined by its unity of religious, dogmatic consciousness, containing and confessing the true faith. This concept of the true faith, of Orthodoxy, cannot be conceived as some abstract norm. On the contrary, true faith has a definite content of dogmatic teaching, which the Church confesses, demanding of its members the same confession. Thus a departure from the true faith means separation from the Church: heresy or schism.

The Incarnation took place in the world, not above it. It completed historic time without destroying human history, but rather giving it a meaning positive and eternal, and becoming its center. In

9

spite of its divine and eternal nature (or, more exactly, because of it) the Church has a history within the boundaries of human history and in connection with it. Christianity is greater than, but not outside, history; it has a history of its own. In this history the Church takes dogmatic forms; it provides the norms of true belief, of the profession of the true faith. And each member of the Church, instead of placing himself outside the history of the Church, accepts the doctrine of the Church, expressed and fixed during all the time of its history. The life of the Church, while mysterious and hidden, does not for that reason become illogical and "non-dogmatic"; on the contrary, it has a logos, a doctrine and a message. The Lord, who is the Way, the Truth and the Life, preached the Gospel of the Kingdom in revealing the meaning of the Scriptures announcing the dogmas concerning Himself, the Father and the Spirit. His Church concerns itself with the same things. For "faith comes from what is heard, and what is heard comes by the preaching of Christ" (Rom. 10:17). Knowledge comes from the preaching of the true faith. Right living is necessarily connected with right believing; they come one from the other.

The fullness of the true faith, the true doctrine, is much too vast to be held in the consciousness of an isolated member of the Church; it is guarded by the whole Church and transmitted from generation to generation, as the tradition of the Church. Tradition is the living memory of the Church, containing the true doctrine that manifests itself in its history. It is not an archeological museum, not a scientific catalogue; it is not, furthermore, a dead depository. No, tradition is a living power inherent in a living organism. In the stream of its life it bears along the past in all its forms so that all the past is contained in the present and is the present. The unity and continuity of tradition follow from the fact that the Church is always identical with itself. The Church has an unique life, guided at all times by the Holy Spirit; the historical form changes, but the spirit remains unchanged. Thus belief in Church tradition as the basic source of Church doctrine arises from a belief in the unity and self-identity of the Church. The period of primitive Christianity is very unlike the present time, yet one must admit that it is the same Church like unto itself; by its unity of life, the Church binds together the communities of Paul and the local Churches of today. In different epochs, it is true, tradition has not been known and comprehended in the same degree by all members of the Church, and it may be said, practically, that tradition is inexhaustible, for it is the very life of the Church. But it remains living and active, even when it continues unknown. The essential principle of tradition is this: each member of the Church, in his life and his knowledge (whether it concerns scientific theology or practical wisdom) should seek to attain the integral unity of tradition, to test himself if he is in accord with it. He ought to carry in himself living tradition; he ought to be a link inseparably connected with all the chain of history.

Tradition has many aspects; it can be written, oral, monumental. Besides, there is one source of tradition which occupies a place apart, perfectly recognized; it is Holy Scripture. Does Scripture or tradition hold the primacy? At the time of the Reformation the Western Church tried to oppose Scripture to tradition; really no such opposition exists. The idea of such antagonism was produced artificially by conflicting desires, either to lessen the value of Scripture in behalf of tradition, or the reverse. Scripture and tradition belong to the one life of the Church moved by the same Holy Spirit, which operates in the Church, manifesting itself in tradition and inspiring sacred writers. In this connection we should note that the latest Bible studies make increasing use of the traditional and collective element. Analysis of the books of the Old and New Testaments, especially the Gospels, has disclosed the early sources from which these books were drawn. Holy Scripture thus becomes a sort of written tradition, and the place for those individual writers who were once thought to have written, so to say, under the dictation of the Holy Spirit becomes less and less. Holy books such as the Epistles of the Apostles — are they other than chronicles of the life of the different churches, preserved by tradition? Scripture and tradition must be comprehended, not as opposed one to the other, but as united, but not identical.

Holy Scripture is thus a part of the tradition of the Church. It is that tradition which affirms the value of the holy books in the Church. The canon of holy books which affirms their inspired character is established by tradition; the inspired nature of the scripture can be guaranteed only by the church, that is to say, by tradition. It is given to each to judge, in accordance with his personal taste, the value and the inspiration of a given work, but no one can of himself decide questions relative to the divine inspiration of the Scriptures and the presence of the Holy Spirit in the Bible. That is given only by the Spirit of God which lives in the Church, for "no one knows divine things, except the Spirit of God." This cannot then be a question of personal choice but depends only on the judgment of the Church. History tells us that among many written works the Church has chosen a small number as inspired by God; among many Gospels it chose the canonical Gospels. After much hesitation, it included in the canon certain books (for example, the Song of Songs, the Apocalypse) and reject others which were a part of them for a certain time (the epistle of Clement, the Shepherd of Hermas); it has maintained the difference between canonical and non-canonical books (deutero-canonical, pseudo-epigraphal and apocryphal). It is right to say that the Word of God possesses an inherent witness to itself, an intrinsic efficacy, a sort of immanent evidence of its inspired character, and it would not be the Word of God, addressed to men, if it did not penetrate into human consciousness like a cutting sword. And yet it would be exaggeration and error to think that a person could, by his own choice and after his own taste, establish that certain written works were inspired; these works he can comprehend only in the measure of his personal capacity, and in a manner of thought characteristic of a given time.

The Church has given us the Bible through tradition, and the Reformers themselves receive the Bible from the Church and by the Church, that is to say, by tradition. It is not for each of us to establish anew the canonicity of Scripture. Each one must discover it for himself, in feeding upon the Word of God, but he must nevertheless receive it as such at the hands of the Church which speaks through tradition. Otherwise Scripture ceases to be the Word of God; it becomes a book, a literary work, subject to philological and historical investigations. But the Word of God, while being studied as an historical document, can never become only a document, for its exterior form, although bearing the character of a certain historic epoch, nevertheless encloses the word of eternal life; in this same sense it is a symbol, the meeting place of divine and human.

We should read the Word of God with faith and veneration, in the spirit of the Church. There cannot be, there should not be, any break between Scripture and tradition. No reader of the Word of God can comprehend for himself the inspired character of that which he reads, for to the individual there is not given an organ of such comprehension. Such an organ is available to the reader only when he finds himself in union with all in the Church. The idea that one can himself discern, at his own risk and peril, the Word of God, that one may become interlocutor of God, is illusory: this Divine Gift is received only from the Church. This gift is received immediately, in its fullness, in union with the Church, in the temple, where the reading of the Word of God is preceded and followed by a special prayer. We there ask God to aid us in hearing His Word and in opening our hearts to His Spirit.

The Divine Word, it is true, can well enter the individual perception, become an individual good, thanks to the inherent efficacy of the Word of God and of its interior evidence; Protestants are right so to affirm. If there were not that individual, direct perception (of the individual in the Church) the Bible would become a sacred fetish, spoken of by the Apostle when he says: "The letter killeth, the spirit giveth life." It is right that there should be this personal discovery of the Word of God, its comprehension by the individual. That comprehension may be immediate or not. It is not immediate when one receives the truths of the Word of God, not directly from the Bible, but by means of the divine service, pictures, preaching, etc. In any case, the personal reception is possible only if one is in spiritual union with the Church, if one feels himself close to the Church, if one participates in its entire life; nevertheless the reception must be an individual matter. And we think that between the Protestant point of view and that of the Orthodox Church there is no real disagreement, only a superficial one. For Protestantism also accepts the canon of the sacred books, as a norm which should be our guide. The reformers wished to have their Bible separated from the Church. But it seems the Bible cannot be separated from the Church, for separated from the Church, it becomes simply a collection of "books," a human document, "writings." The Church, then, gives us the Bible as the Word of God, in the canon of the sacred books, and ecclesiastical tradition bears witness to it. Only the transcendent can testify to transcendence. The Church, which encloses in itself the divine life united to human things, speaks of that which is divine, especially of the divine character of the Word of God. As for the individual, he may or may not be in the Church, but he is not himself the Church. In the history of the Church the recognition of the Word of God and a statement of that fact is the origin of the canon of the sacred books. The canon, however, does not order, by some exterior law, the recognition or non-recognition of certain sacred books; it testifies rather to the fact that the Church has already accepted them. It declares, confirms and legalizes that acceptance which cannot from henceforth be doubted. The ecclesiastical power, the councils of bishops, which express the knowledge of the Church, have only to give a true expression, an unchangeable formulation to that which already exists in the life of the Church, to that which is given by the Holy Spirit guiding that life.

And here a council operates not at all as an authority, but as an organ of the Church, as its head. And only after this solemn proclamation of the truth already accepted by the Church, the canon of the holy books becomes the norm of ecclesiastical life, a law to which the individual conscience should be adjusted.

Ecclesiastical tradition is always being created; the process never stops. It is not only the past, but also the present. Touching the canon, the ancient Church formulated its definitions only under the most general forms, replying to questions which arose then: which are the books forming part of the Word of God and which are those not a part of it? The Church thus established only a sort of general catalogue of Scripture. Its decisions have absolute authority concerning what is excluded from or not included in the canon. It is a negative judgment, clear and simple, which certainly has primary importance. The positive verdict, on the contrary, gives only a very general judgment as to the indication of the character of divine inspiration, which differs among the books. It says nothing about the immediate authorship of the books of the canon, which in certain cases do not correspond to their titles (for example, the Pentateuch, at least in certain parts, many Psalms, Proverbs, the Book of Wisdom, etc.; in the New Testament, the synoptic Gospels from the point of view of original sources). Nothing is said on the question of inspiration itself, of the correlation of divine and human which works in these books, of their history, nor of the interpretation of the relationship between their content and their historical background. In a word, the whole domain of Old and New Testament science—isagogic, critical, hermeneutic—which has received scientific study so fruitful and in many respects so unexpected: this domain is still far from being completely explored, it is still nothing but a domain of open questions, it is the domain of living tradition which is being created.

We also, follow the march of history, and the Word of God seems to evolve according to our understanding. It does not change in its eternal content, but in the form accessible to human comprehension. Thus tradition, at the point of crystallization represented by the definitions of the Church, even in regard to the Word of God, is never finished and exhausted. Once fixed, tradition certainly becomes obligatory in the very measure of its authenticity and demands that great attention be given it, particularly for the traditional attribution of the sacred books to one or another author. It is impossible to ignore these attributions; it is even necessary to accept them in a certain sense, but it is not necessary to take them literally, as we do authors of our own day. The Church does not ob-

ject to the study of the Word of God by all means possible, particularly by the methods of scientific contemporary criticism; more,
it does not decide beforehand on the findings of that criticism, provided only that a pious and religious sentiment is preserved toward
the sacred text as toward the Word of God. On the one hand it is impossible in Orthodoxy to have a rationalistic criticism, without
faith, without religious principles, entirely detached from religion, a
criticism which decomposes everything and which abolishes "the
method of veneration." Such rationalism has made itself felt in
liberal Protestantism, but it now seems to be becoming less extreme
and returning to the way of tradition. On the other hand it is not
possible in Orthodoxy to have an exegetic discipline imposed from
without, such as the "Biblical Commission" of Rome. With us
there is no place for a "Biblical Commission" which by its decisions pretends to bind and direct scientific study, forgetting that
science enslaved is not science and is worth nothing. Orthodoxy affords liberty for scientific study, provided the fundamental dogmas
of the Church and the ecclesiastical definitions are safeguarded; it
would be inadmissible, for scientific reasons, to change the canon of
the holy books, to abrogate or to add to it. If the divinity of Our
Lord is not accepted, His miracles, His Resurrection, the Holy
Trinity—scientific study becomes tainted by an interior imperfec-
tion; it becomes blind and opinionated concerning all the Scriptures
where these points are touched upon.

Such a science of the Word of God, a science without faith, contradicts itself. This internal contradiction affects equally all attempts
to establish "scientifically" by means of historical criticism the
veritable essence of Christianity, "das Wesen des Christentums,"
outside the Church and its tradition. Thus a hopeless confusion
arises between different domains, a confusion which, in advance,
condemns scientific studies to religious sterility. It must be admitted
from the very first that ecclesiastical science, while completely free
and sincere, is not without premises (*Voraussetzungslos*), but a
science dogmatically conditioned, a science of things believed or
not. In this it is like the rationalistic science of unbelievers, which

proceeds also from certain dogmatic but negative premises. Thus, for example, it is not possible, while retaining full liberty of scientific criticism, to study the Gospel stories of the Resurrection of Christ, if one has not an exact dogmatic attitude upon the fact of the Resurrection (belief or unbelief). Such is the nature of a science dealing with belief. That science is not so difficult for those who do not believe as for those who half believe; the latter take as a decisive criterion their personal point of view, detached from ecclesiastical tradition. This is the position of certain extreme forms of liberal Protestantism, while Anglican theology often shows a complete scientific independence which does not hinder it at all from remaining true to the teaching of the Church. In this aspect the Biblical science of Anglicans corresponds better to the demands of Orthodoxy. Because of certain historic circumstances, Orthodox Biblical science has not yet developed in such a way as to furnish independent models and norms of Biblical theology. This science remains, on the whole, the special heritage of Protestant or Anglican peoples. Catholic science concerns itself above all with defensive apologetics. Free Orthodox Biblical science, which began to develop in the nineteenth century in Russia, belongs mainly to the future. But there is no reason why it should not profit by scientific results achieved in modern times by the western Christian world—on the contrary, it is entirely natural thus to profit. After having corrected and completed such results, they can be introduced into ecclesiastical tradition; this would in no wise abrogate the latter, but elucidate and complete what already exists. The truth is one, but men learn to know it by the discursive processes of development. And the Orthodox consciousness has neither to fear nor to be disturbed by Biblical criticism, for, by means of that criticism, there is gained a more exact idea of the ways of God and the action of the Holy Spirit, which has operated in the Church in different times and in different ways.

Orthodoxy has no reason to shun the modern scientific spirit, when it is a question of genuine research and not of giving free rein to the prejudices of an epoch; on the contrary, that scientific spirit belongs to Orthodoxy as does everything living and active in human history. Orthodoxy has a universal scale; it cannot be measured by one epoch only, which would give it an exclusive and particular imprint. It includes and unites everything truly creative, for the hidden promptings of real creativeness and of real knowledge proceed only from the Spirit of God Who lives in the Church.

Ecclesiastical tradition gives testimony to Scripture, and Scripture is itself a part of tradition, but its uniqueness is not thus lessened; it preserves its own nature as the Word of God. Known anew and guaranteed by tradition, it lives as an independent and primary source of faith and doctrine. The inclusion of Holy Scripture in tradition by no means compromises its originality and its value as the Word of God; the Word of God is above all other sources of faith, especially of all tradition in all its forms. Tradition adapts itself to the different needs of different epochs; Holy Scripture, that is the voice of God addressed to man, has absolute value, though revealed under a conditioned historic form. It is the eternal revelation of divinity, a revelation addressed not only to this age but to the ages to come, and not only to the world of men but to that of angels, the eternal good tidings of the angel who flew in the midst of heaven (Rev. 14:6). From this point of view, it must be said that Holy Scripture and tradition are unequal in value. First place belongs to the Word of God; the criterion of the truth of Scripture is not tradition (although tradition testifies to Scripture), but on the contrary, tradition is recognized when founded on Scripture. Tradition cannot be in disagreement with Scripture. Statements are sometimes encountered which put the decisions of the first four ecumenical councils on the same level as the four Gospels (e.g., Pope Gregory the Great), but these are only an exaggerated and oratorical eulogy of the value of conciliar decisions, eulogy which certainly should not be taken literally. Tradition always supports itself by Scripture; it is an interpretation of Scripture. The germ found in Scripture is the seed; tradition is the harvest which pushes through the soil of human history.

The Word of God is at the same time the word of man, which contains the inspiration of the Holy Spirit; it has been, so to speak, uttered by Him. It has become of the same nature as the God-Man, divine and human at the same time. In whatever fashion inspiration is understood, it must always be admitted that its human form depends upon historical circumstances, such as language, time, national character. Contemporary Biblical science is learning more and more to distinguish this historical form, and thus we increase our comprehension of the concrete side of inspiration. But although dependent upon historical circumstance, Scripture always preserves its divine power, since the Word of the God-Man, the Word of God addressed to man, could be spoken only in human language. But that human historical form becomes an obstacle to the understanding of the Word of God; it becomes transparent only under the guidance of the Spirit of God, Who lives in the Church, so that to understand the inspired Scripture a special inspiration, inherent only in the Church, is necessary.

Holy Scripture, the Bible, was compiled in the course of centuries from among books by various authors, of different epochs, of different content, of different degrees of revelation. This is true of the two Testaments; the Old, which is no longer valid as a covenant, and the New, which is not yet completely manifested. The Bible is not a system, but a conglomerate, a mosaic in which the divine word is written by the hand of God. It is like the fantastic creations of natural forces which raise the surface of the earth to form chains of mountains, which again lower it to form the bottom of the sea. This is why the Bible does not have a finished, exterior form or system. The canon of the holy books has been formed by ecclesiastical definitions, but that is only an exterior fact; it possesses the force of a fact, and not that of interior self-evidence. The fullness of the Word of God does not consist in an external ''finish'' of its form (this it does not have), but in its interior fullness, which is manifested in inseparable connection with the Church tradition. The Church has always lived under the guidance of the Holy Spirit, it has always possessed the fullness inherent in it; nevertheless it has not always had the Bible, at least in its present form. The books of the Old Testament came into it as they took form, and not all at once. The Church of the New Testament, during the first flourishing days of its existence, lived entirely without sacred books, without even the Gospels; these were produced only in the course of the first century, and were made part of the canon, together with the Epistles much later, finally taking definite form at the beginning of the fourth century. This shows that it is the Holy Spirit, living in the Church, which is essential, and not one or another of its manifestations. It must be added that the content of the Word of God differs in its different parts, both as to the general purpose of the books (law, historical books, books of instruction, prophetic books, Gospels, Epistles, Apocalypse), and as to their own substance. Although all the Bible is the Word of God, ''all Scripture is inspired by God'' (2 Tim. 3:16), we distinguish among its parts those more or less important for us, at least within the limits of that which is accessible to us. The Gospels are for us different from the books of Ruth or Joshua; the Epistles are not the same as Ecclesiastes or Proverbs. The same distinction obtains between canonical and deutero-canonical books.

Protestantism has arbitrarily impoverished its Bible by excluding the deutero-canonical books; this is beginning to be understood now and there is a tendency to give them again their value. This distinction in degree of divine inspiration seems contradictory. Can there be degrees of inspiration? Is there not simply presence or absence of inspiration? This simply means that divine inspiration is concrete and that it adapts itself to human weakness and consequently can be greater or less. This is why the non-canonical books have a certain authority as the Word of God, but less authority than that of the canonical books. Generally speaking, the Bible is an entire universe, it is a mysterious organism, and it is only partially that we attain to living in it. The Bible is inexhaustible for us because of its divine content and its composition, its many aspects; by reason, also, of our limited and changing mentality. The Bible is a heavenly constellation, shining above us eternally, while we move on the sea of human existence. We gaze at that constellation, and it remains fixed, but it is also continually changes its place in relation to us.

It is highly important to establish a right relationship between the Word of God and tradition in the life of the Church. The Word of God may be considered as the unique and primary source of Christian doctrine, and "Biblicalism" as the truest manifestation of the ecclesiastical spirit (this is the case in Protestantism). In this case Christianity becomes the religion of a book instead of being that of spirit and of life—the religion of the New Testament scribes. But the Bible, considered solely as a book, ceases to be the Bible, which it can be only in the Church. Biblical orthodoxy, which is developed in certain branches of Protestantism and in certain sects, dries up Christianity, making of it a legalistic religion. Catholicism of the Middle Ages neglected Bible reading; it had no confidence in such reading, which produced a direct "anti-Biblicalism." Certainly, each member of the Church has the right to possess the Bible. In fact, the degree of Biblicalism in a church corresponds to its level of ecclesiastical culture. This varies among different peoples, and, in this particular, first place belongs to Protestantism. To forbid the reading of the Bible to laymen, nowadays, would be heresy. As a matter of fact no Church does forbid it. But, the connection between Scripture and tradition being so close, a man not knowing the Bible cannot be considered as deprived of Christian instruction, where the vacancy is filled by living tradition: oral, cultural, plastic. And just as the Church, at its best moments, has had the power to exist without the written word, certain communities continue to live without the Scriptures in our day. A Christian can and should have a personal attitude towards the Bible, a life united with the Bible, just as he should have an individual prayer-life. This personal connection comes from long years of frequent reading of the Word of God. We have examples of this among the Fathers of the Church whose speech was impregnated with Biblical expressions. They thought in terms of the Bible—lived with it. The Word of God became an inexhaustible source of instruction. But such a personal feeling toward the Bible does not remain individual and isolated or lose its connection with the Church. The attitude of the Church does not extinguish the personal sentiment; on the contrary, it somehow makes it more definite. For all that is ecclesiastical lives only in that which is personal, and it is in the union of the individual and the collective that the mystery lies, which is the spirit of the Church.

The Word of God is used in the Church in two ways: liturgically and non-liturgically. In the first instance the Bible is used not simply in separate readings, but is made part of the daily rite. This liturgical reading gives a passage a special value. The event whose story is read happens in spirit in the Church; it is not an account of something which happened in the past and no longer exists but also the event itself. Such are, for example, the readings about the Gospel events, especially on great feast days. The Church mystically relives the happening itself, and the reading of the Gospel has the force of an event. This is why the liturgical reading of the Word of God is possible only in the Church, and nowhere outside. Such reading is of the greatest importance, because the living force of the Word of God is there manifested. Such liturgical use is possible only with certain chosen portions of the Word of God, above all with the New Testament, but it by no means excludes the possibility of penetrating the meaning of Scripture outside the service. This latter needs specially to be guided by Church tradition.

When Scripture is read outside the service, it is necessary, from the very first, to discriminate between the scientific point of view and the religious. It is not that these points of view mutually exclude or oppose each other, but that each of them makes its special emphasis. The scientific study of Scripture, as a work of literature, differs not at all from other categories of scientific study. The same methods are used. The results of scientific study are inevitably and naturally applied to the religious interpretation of the content of the Word of God in so far as they help to attain a more exact understanding of its historic form.

Scientific study, while maintaining full liberty in its own limited domain, cannot pretend to interpret Scripture from the point of view of dogma—and yet this often happens. Still this scientific study does partake, in a certain degree, of dogmatic exegesis. In reality, knowledge of the sacred text, under all its possible aspects, has necessarily a certain value for religious interpretation. Consequently scientific study itself, scientific tradition, now begins to form a part of the general Church tradition regarding the interpretation of Scripture. A scholar cannot begin his work by taking himself as his sole point of departure. He must study the work of all his predecessors and carry it on without a break in the continuity. Thus it is equally impossible that an interpreter of Scripture, working to understand the religious point of view, should ignore the results of scientific study already made, without prejudice, even if he does not accept all such results. Thanks to contemporary scientific study the sacred text may be seen anew; what may be called the scientific tradition is normal and inevitable. This tradition, by the way dates from the most ancient times, beginning with the interpreters of the ''Septuagint,'' the Great Synagogue and the Holy Fathers.

The Church then applies to the interpretation of Scripture this self-evident general principle: the understanding of Holy Scripture must be based on tradition. In other words, when one undertakes to understand the Word of God from the point of view of faith and dogma, one must necessarily be in accord with the interpretation of the Church handed down by the divinely-inspired Fathers and teachers of the Church and from the apostolic times. After His resurrection Our Lord opened to His disciples the understanding of the Scriptures (Luke 24:45). This understanding continues to be opened to us by the action of the Holy Spirit in the Church. Thus the treasure of wisdom of the Church is formed; not to use it would be folly. This principle curbs the individual will by placing man face to face with the Church, subordinating him interiorly to the control of tradition, making him responsible, not only as an isolated individual, but also as a member of the Church. In practice, it amounts to this: in obvious cases his conception of certain events or doctrines must not be in disagreement with the fundamental conceptions of the Church. In less obvious cases he is obliged to collate his opinions with what predominates in Church tradition; he must himself seek such verification and agreement. For the spirit which lives in the Church is one—it is the spirit of unity and not of discord.

This principle by no means excludes a personal feeling toward the Word of God, or the individual effort to understand it. On the contrary, when the individual does not apply himself personally to the Word of God, it remains a closed book. But this individual feeling must not be egotistically individual; it must be full of the "spirit of the Church." We must be, within ourselves, in union with the Church and feel keenly our "sonship" in the unique life of the unique Spirit. If then we aspire to be connected with Church tradition, this is a natural need springing from free personal feelings, for liberty is not license of free will, but love and concord.

In practice, after having found the testimony of tradition, the exegetist ought to connect his own opinion with such testimony, and to try to place his opinion in the context of interpretation given by the Church. Scientific study also tends to understand each question in connection with its history; in this sense, science also seeks a sort of tradition in history. But for science, history is rather a succession of exterior events than a unique manifestation of the spirit which lives in it; it is more the history of errors than a testimony to the truth. And yet the difference in the point of view of the separate communions in regard to tradition is often exaggerated. It is thought that Protestantism denies all tradition because it accepts this only in limited fashion, and denies certain particular traditions—which do not always correspond with the tradition of the whole Church. Protestantism began by denying the primacy of the Pope, indulgences, etc., and came at last to reject all tradition. This contradiction will be softened if it is taken into consideration that in fact the Church tradition concerning certain questions (for example the exegesis of certain texts, such as Matt. 16:18) is not an entirely exterior order (such as those of the Biblical Commission of Rome) but rather an unknown quantity which one must search and find, and decide for oneself. For tradition, in regard to one or another question, is not expressed in some Church rule obligatory for all, which is the result of a conflict of opinions (like the definitions of the Councils) but includes opinions of great authority and of different shades of meaning, sometimes even contradictory. The differences of exegesis and of method in ecclesiastical writers are too well known to be overlooked. If a guide is sought in tradition, it must be accepted not as an external norm or an order, but as an internal and creative work. In the Roman Church where the Pope is living tradition, there is no place for such a creative attitude toward tradition, for the meaning of tradition here is that which the Pope attributes to it. Such a state of affairs does not exist in Orthodoxy, and fidelity to tradition expresses itself by the tendency to be in accord with the spirit of the doctrine of the Church in so far as that spirit is evident in a given case.

This fidelity, consequently, does not shut out liberty and the creative spirit, but even presupposes them. It is not a substitute for a personal understanding and by no means does away with such understanding, but only enriches it.

Tradition is not a law, it is not legalistic literalism; it is unity in the spirit, in faith and in truth. It is natural and appropriate to the conscience of the Church, while proud individualism and egocentrism are contrary to the Church's nature and spirit. As Scripture is given to the Church and by the Church, it must be comprehended also in the spirit of the Church, that is in connection with ecclesiastical tradition and not outside it. But the fact remains that God has given us a thought of our own, and that our personal work cannot be done in the past. In other words, ecclesiastical tradition does not put the voice of the past in the place of the voice of the present; in it the past does not kill the present, but gives it full force. That it is necessary to follow ecclesiastical tradition and to seek in it one's own individuality, to drink of the source of the Church unity, is an axiom of Church consciousness. If the Church is, and if the Word of God is confided to it, it is evident that the perception of truth is given to us as members of the Church and that we, in consequence, ought to preserve the spirit of the Church.

Fidelity to tradition in that which concerns the divine word—

such is the spirit of the Church. It is now time to consider the general dogmatic question: what is tradition?

The Nature of Church Tradition

The tradition of the Church is an exterior, phenomenal manifestation of the interior, noumenal unity of the Church. It must be comprehended as a living force, as the consciousness of one organism, in which all its previous life is included. Thus tradition is uninterrupted and inexhaustible; it is not only the past, but also the present, in which the future lives, as well. We have an image of living tradition in the relationship between Old and New Testaments. The Old Testament is not abrogated, but completed, by the New. Still the Old contains the New within itself in a preparatory form, as its own fulfilment, its own future. And from the New Testament there stream rays of light into the new age, beyond the Second Coming—light which extends from the Creator to the Fulfilment when He shall be "all in all."

Tradition is not a sort of archeology, which by its shadows connects the present with the past, nor a law—it is the fact that the life of the Church remains always identical with itself. Tradition receives a "normative" value precisely because of this identity. And as the same spirit dwells in each man living the life of the Church, he is not limited to touching the surface of tradition, but, in so far as he is filled with the spirit of the Church, he enters into it. But the measure of that spirit is also the measure of sanctity. This is why sanctity is an interior norm used to determine what constitutes Church tradition. The light of sanctity thus illuminates tradition.

From an exterior point of view, tradition expresses itself by all that is impregnated with the Spirit of the Church, and in this sense it is inexhaustible. Into the personal conscience of each member of the Church there enters only a drop of that sea, a grain of that treasure. But here, quality matters more than quantity. The timid and trembling light of a candle lighted at the sacred flame preserves that same flame. The candles burning in the temple whose many lights transform themselves into one light, represent Church tradition as diffused in the entire Church.

In the interior life of the Church, its tradition assumes many forms, literary, liturgical, canonical documents, and memorials. All the life of the Church at all times in its existence, as far as it is fixed in documents—this is Church tradition.

Tradition is not a book which records a certain moment in the development of the Church and stops itself, but a book always being written by the Church's life. Tradition continues always and now not less than before; we live in tradition and create it. And nevertheless the sacred tradition of the past exists for us as present; it lives in our own life and consciousness. Moreover, between the past and the present there is this difference, that the present is for us fluid and without form, still being created, while the tradition of the past is offered to our knowledge under forms already crystallized, accessible to intelligence.

Tradition concerns faith and life, doctrine and piety. Primitive tradition was oral—Our Lord Himself wrote nothing and taught His disciples by word of mouth, and primitive teaching was also oral. But little by little tradition became written. In practice, the Church picks out from the written body of tradition the most essential parts and gives them the force of ecclesiastical law (the Canon), their acceptance and acknowledgement become obligatory for all Christians. Such a minimum of tradition obligatory for all, but by no means exhausting all tradition, the Church has forced from the decisions of the Councils, ecumenical and local, possessing most authority, supreme organs of the ecclesiastical power of an epoch. Such a profession of faith, obligatory for all, is the Nicene Creed recited during the liturgy (to which may be added the Apostles' Creed, which has less value and is not of liturgical use, and especially the Athanasian Creed). Then come the dogmatic definitions of the seven ecumenical councils. Anyone who does not accept this minimum of Church tradition by that fact separates himself from the society of the Church. The canons of the ecumenical and local councils, concerning various sides of the life of the church, are also obligatory. But the value and importance of these practical rules cannot be compared with the dogmatic definitions mentioned above, many among them being the outcome of historic circumstances. Thus certain canons have been simply abrogated by others more recent (something which cannot happen to dogmatic definitions); other canons, without being formally abrogated, are no longer in force. Ceasing to be living tradition in the Church, they enter the domain of history and of archeology. But it is just upon these ecclesiastical laws which are based upon tradition, that the organization of the Church and the hierarchical order rests. Regarding Church services, a ruling also obligatory for all is the so-called Typicon which fixes all the services during the entire ecclesiastical year. But the Typicon, also, does not have the value of the dogmatic canons. Its requirements change according to varying conditions of life and place; it is obligatory only in a general manner. In principle the order of service can assume different forms, as happened, for example, before the separation of the Church, when there were two rites—Eastern and Western—and two liturgies, each of equal value, though such differences in regard to dogma were of course not permitted. And when such difference appeared in regard to the procession of the Holy Spirit ("filioque"), it led to separation. All the order of the services and the sacraments belongs especially to the domain of Church tradition—written and oral—and both are equally obligatory.

By means of the services certain dogmas of Christian doctrine which have not been declared by the definitions of the ecumenical councils, acquire the force of law. For example: reverence of the Mother of God in Orthodoxy, the doctrine of the Seven Sacraments, the cult of holy images and relics, the teachings about the future life, many things which liturgical tradition suggests for our acceptance, in a manner sometimes more powerful than conciliar decision. Thus the dogmatic definitions of the Councils of Constantinople of the fourteenth century concerning the doctrine of Gregory Palamas about the light on Mt. Tabor are confirmed by the services of the second week of Lent; on the other hand, the definitions of the Councils of Constantinople of the seventeenth century on transubstantiation, which are not confirmed liturgically, have not the same authority.

The maxim of St. Vincent de Lerins on tradition: "quod semper, quod ubique, quod ab omnibus traditum est"—is often considered as a guiding rule on the subject. Nevertheless, this principle, systematically applied, cannot have the universal importance which is sometimes attributed to it. First this maxim excludes all possibility of the historic origin of new dogmatic formulas (this includes even the pronouncements of the seven ecumenical councils), for they do not agree with the "semper" of the maxim. So, to demand that tradition should be ecumenical quantitatively—ab omnibus et ubique—does not seem to correspond to the essentials of things, for then local traditions would become impossible (and nevertheless these traditions can, in the course of time, become universal). Besides, it can happen that the truth of the Church is professed not by a majority but by the minority of members (for example, at the time of Arianism). In general the above maxim makes impossible all movement in Church tradition, which is nevertheless movement itself; the life of the Church would be condemned to immobility, and its history would become superfluous and even impertinent. This is why the maxim of Vincent de Lérins, understood formally, does not correspond at all with the whole of the life of the Church. Thus it can be accepted only in a limited and relative sense, in the sense that true dogmas, already proclaimed by the Church as such, are obligatory for all. The point in question here concerns the definitions of the seven ecumenical councils; their denial would be truly in contradiction—direct or indirect—with the profession of faith which is the foundation stone of the Church: "You are the Christ, the Son of the living God" (Matt. 16:17). To the maxim of Vincent de Lerins must be added the word ascribed to St. Augustine: "In necessariis unitas, in dubiis libertas, in omnibus caritas." This latter maxim better expresses the real life of tradition where one part which is certain and already manifest must be distinguished from another part which is not yet so revealed and in that sense doubtful, or problematic.

Outside this part of tradition fixed by the Church as lex credendi or lex orandi, or lex canonica or lex ecclesiastica, there remains a vast domain of tradition which has not the same clearness and remains a problem for theological knowledge and science. The monuments of Church tradition are, first of all, ecclesiastical literature in the wide acceptance of the word: the works of the Apostolic Fathers, the Fathers of the Church, the theologians. Afterwards come liturgical texts, architecture, iconography, ecclesiastical art; finally usage and oral tradition. All this tradition, while produced by the same unique Spirit Who lives in the Church, is at the same time impregnated with historic relativity and human narrowness. On certain points of detail, differences, divergencies and contradictions are permitted. All these gifts of tradition should be studied, compared, understood. It seems necessary, in depending upon the monuments of tradition, to fix upon what can truly be called the tradition of the Church. The measure of the plenitude of this comprehension may vary. Certain epochs can have a more or less sharp perception of different aspects of the doctrine of the Church. Then, all that preserves the living memory of the Church forms the volume of tradition. The quality of ecclesiastical tradition is the unique life of the Church, guided by the Holy Spirit in all times. The life of tradition consists in the inexhaustible creative work of the Church by which the depths of its knowledge are manifested. Thus Church tradition is the life of the Church in the past which is also the present. It is a divine truth revealed in human words, deeds, and decisions. It is the divine-human body of the Church, living in space and time. Least of all it is external, obligatory law, which is only a small part of tradition. It is rather an inner law of the Church, arising from its unity.

Is the Church capable of historic development, particularly of dogmatic development? This is the question which presents itself on the subject of Church tradition as history. On the one hand this question is answered by the facts themselves, for it is obvious that dogmas are developed in history and that, in consequence, the Church knows a development of dogma. The primitive Church, in comparison with the epoch of the ecumenical councils, was comparatively adogmatic, and the contemporary Church is richer and more full of dogmatic "content" than the ancient Church. But on the other hand, the Holy Spirit, Who resides in the Church and the external life which He gives us, knows neither diminution nor augmentation, and thus the Church is always identical with itself, without evolutional change. This apparent contradiction arises from the fact that the Church is the union, at the same time, of human and divine life; its substance is invariable in its plenitude and its identity with itself, but its human element lives and develops in time, lives not only with the grace-endowed life of the Church, but also with the life of the world. The leaven of the Kingdom of God is mixed with a dough which ferments according to its own laws. The historical development of the Church consists in a realization of its super-historic content; it is, so to say, a translation of the language of eternity into that of human history, a translation which—notwithstanding the unchangeableness of its content—nevertheless reflects the peculiarities of a given epoch and language; it is a varying form, more or less adequate, for an invariable content. In this sense it is possible to speak of dogmatic development, and just on this account it is equally impossible to speak of stagnation or immobility in the consciousness of the Church.

Dogmatic definitions are made with the means and content of a given epoch and thus these definitions reflect the style and the peculiarities of that epoch. The Christological controversies and the definitions of the ecumenical councils most certainly reflect the spirit of Greek thought. These are, in a certain sense, translations of the fundamental truth of the Church into the Hellenistic tongue. Even contemporary dogmatic controversies, in matters of ecclesiology, for instance, are marked by the spirit of modern times and its philosophy. That is to say, the expression of dogmatic formulas is determined by historic circumstances, so to speak, pragmatically. This does not lessen their significance but merely indicates their connection with the inevitable historic development of the Church. Dogmas arise from the need to understand anew and to reinterpret anew the elements of the experience of the Church. This is why, in principle, new dogmatic definitions will always be possible. In fact, in the thought of the Church, new thoughts and new dogmatic definitions are always ripening, while the unique and divine life of the Church remains always identical with itself, outside of and above history.

Let us distinguish between that part of Church tradition which remains absolutely unchanged and that in which a certain development is possible. The Spirit of God living in the Church never changes, neither does Christ Himself, but on the other hand we must clearly recognize the inevitability of dogmatic development in the revelation of Church consciousness, since certain of its expressions are of purely historical origin and pragmatic in character. This recognition of pragmatism or historism in dogmatic development, and hence in dogmatic forms, in no wise diminishes the significance of dogma. It does not introduce a general historic relativism, according to which dogmas may not only arise, but grow old and die. Relativism relates to forms and not to content. As to the latter, it partakes of the unity and constancy of tradition. It cannot be abrogated, and in this sense, the content of dogma is without fault and, so to speak, absolute. But though content is absolute, form is not, although we should recognize the higher appropriateness of a given form and its content. For instance, Greek philosophy was accepted as the most satisfactory form for the expression of Christology. This pragmatism of form is nevertheless no hindrance to the special divine inspiration which, so the Church holds, is evident in the dogmatic decisions of the ecumenical councils. We should remember that the Word of God has its historic external form, belonging to a definite historical epoch, bearing the marks of time, yet in no way thereby losing its divine inspiration. On the other hand, we must not identify the dogmatic formulas of Church tradition, formulas of historic origins, with the Word of God which bears within itself its own absoluteness and eternity. If, for instance, we trace the development in Church literature of the trinitarian formula, we shall see that some writers, even the most authoritative, give it an approximate and inexact expression, which we can accept only in its historic sense. Of course, in this connection, the dogmatic definitions of the ecumenical councils rise above the rest like mountain peaks, although even these, for their complete understanding, demand an historical as well as spiritual commentary.

All Church tradition consists of such relative—absolute, pragmatic, historically-conditioned expressions of the one life of the Church. This means that it must always be historically comprehended in its expression and in its unity, perceived from within. This means, also, that tradition is never completed, but continues such throughout history. Our epoch, our life, in so far as they are in union with the Church, are the continuation of tradition. It results from this, also, that tradition, to be the true tradition of the Church, should be a living tradition. This means we should live it in our lives. To make living tradition a personal inspiration and an effort of the spiritual life are necessary. Tradition is not something static, but something dynamic; it is lit at the fire of our enthusiasm. The scribes and the Pharisees of all epochs would transform tradition into dead archeology, or into an exterior law, into the letter that kills. But the power of tradition is not at all in such a spirit (even in the instances where the law demands that tradition be submitted to): to accept tradition interiorly, to receive it in one's heart—that is what makes the force of tradition. Nothing is more false than the idea, prevalent in the West, of the Eastern Church as the Church of tradition, a church frozen into an immobility of ritualism and traditionalism. If such a spirit exists anywhere, it is only a proof of partial feebleness, of local decadence; it corresponds not at all to the very essence of tradition which is the inexhaustible torrent of the life of the Church, to be understood only by a life of creative effort.

In this sense tradition must be creative; it cannot be otherwise, for the creative effort of our life revives in us all the strength and all the depth of tradition. This act of creation is not personal, individualistic—but it is the act of the Church, an act Catholic, it is the very witness of the Spirit Who lives in the Church.

Tradition contains the truth of the Church, in so far as it is revealed and given for the direction of the Church life, and although it still continues in revelation at the present, yet for every given epoch the infallibility and unchangeability natural to the Church in general are also inherent in it. Infallibility of which the Vatican dogma speaks, even if not very clearly, is only a certain quality of the truth, of life or of life in the truth, natural to the Church; the truth of the dogmatic knowledge of the Church is consonant with that true life.

Infallibility, then, is not theoretical and abstract; it is not the criterion of knowledge, but is a testimony borne to the practical truth of life, practical truth from which flows the truth of dogma as the object of knowledge. "Primum vivere deinde philosophari." In this sense, all the life of the Church is one and the same truth, in spite of differences in its dogmatic formulas. It was the same in the time of primitive Christianity, when all the dogma of the Church was comprised in the profession of faith of St. Peter, and at the time of the ecumenical councils with their complicated theology, as well as in our own day. Heresy is not a dogmatic error, but a corruption of that true life, from which follows a falling-away from the unity of the Church in dogmatic consciousness as well. The sufficiency or fullness of Church tradition does not mean that, as something finished, complete, it cannot be added to, but that the doctrine taught by the Church is always sufficient for true life, for salvation. Each epoch of Church history is complete for itself, not defective, feels no need of any additions to enable its life in God. And fullness and infallibility are only other ways of stating the fact that the Church contains the true life and is the pillar and confirmation of the truth. Unity of tradition is established by unity of life, and unity of tradition establishes unity of faith which is witness to the unity of the Church. What connection is there between the profession of faith and all ecclesiastical tradition? The profession of faith is a brief expression of the content of tradition. This expression is made effective by the organs of the Church, the ecclesiastical councils or the organs of episcopal authority. It takes, then, the power of an ecclesiastical definition; the infallibility and the changelessness inherent in the Church become characteristic of it.[1] How that profession is determined is a question of fact. We have here to elucidate a question of principle, what is the organ of this infallible judgment? Does it exist in the Church? This leads us to study the question of hierarchy in the Church.

---

[1] In recent times there has appeared the idea of ''symbolic books'' or ''confessions'' of Orthodoxy which, like the symbolic books in Protestantism, are supposed to expound the dogmatic constitution or basic law of the Church. Certain documents called by that name (the answer of the Eastern patriarchs to Pius IX, the profession of orthodox faith of Moghila, etc.) may have more or less authority. Nevertheless, they are not symbols of faith: symbolic books, in the strict sense of the word, have no place in Orthodoxy. If they existed, they would replace and abolish the living tradition they are supposed to express. The symbolic books of Protestantism are constitutional charts which serve as foundation for new ecclesiastical societies who do not accept tradition for themselves. Strictly speaking, these books make a beginning of Church tradition for Protestant societies. It is evident that, in this sense, symbolic books are not characteristic of Orthodoxy. What answer to that name are simply the responses of the hierarchy to questions asked by Protestants, or definitions of Orthodoxy, given by itself, as evidence in relation to another confession. Thus pragmatically, and in a certain historic context, these writings also can certainly be submitted to revision.

CHAPTER 3

THE HIERARCHY
Its Nature

St. Paul (1Cor. 12) develops the thought that the Church is the body of Christ, composed of different members. All these members, while of equal value, like the members of the same body, differ as to their place and function; hence, gifts differ, and ministries, but the Spirit is one. In these words St. Paul announces the general principles of the hierarchic and ecclesiastical construction of society. The hierarchical basis, not denying but rather realizing general equality of all, in the presence of natural and spiritual differentiation, is natural to every society with basically spiritual purposes. All the more, then, is it natural to the society which is the Church. The Lord Himself laid the foundations of the hierarchy of the New Alliance when He called the Twelve Apostles, when He initiated them into the mysteries of His teaching and made them witnesses of His life. Each Apostle was called personally by Our Lord to the apostolic ministry. By this fact each received the apostolic dignity, but, at the same time, the Twelve together formed a certain unity—the assembly of the Apostles—which, after the fall of Judas, was reestablished by a new election (Acts 1:15-26). Within the limits of the Twelve, Our Lord sometimes made distinctions, choosing three or four Apostles (Peter, James, John and sometimes Andrew) to be present on the Mount of the Transfiguration or at the place of prayer in the Garden of Gethsemane. Above all, He distinguished two Apostles: Peter and John. Peter is a sort of leader in the assembly of the Apostles; it is he who answers in the name of all in regard to the profession of faith on the road to Caesarea Philippi; it is he who generally appears as the senior of the Apostles. John, the Beloved Disciple, as the result of personal intimacy, was nearest Our Lord during the Last Supper; it is he whom Our Lord on the Cross named as the adopted son of the Holy Virgin. This special mention of Peter and John certainly did not nullify their equality with the other Apostles; neither is invested with a dignity superior to that of the others, as is claimed by the Catholic doctrine of the primacy of St. Peter. But their prominence brings a principle of organization into the mutual relationships of the apostolic group and gives a hieratic constitution to the apostolic hierarchy itself, which serves as prototype for the hieratic relations between equal bishops. This may be observed again in the distinction of James, Cephas and John, considered as pillars by St. Paul (Gal. 2:9). The constitution of the assembly of the Apostles, in spite of the equality of its members, may be compared to the universal Episcopate: in this, side by side with bishops, there are patriarchs, and among these certain priorities exist, or even a unique priority—priority of honor and not of rank, certainly. Our Lord not only singled out the Apostles by their calling, He especially consecrated them by His priestly prayer (John 17), by sending them the Holy Spirit, by His breath. He gave them power to remit sins (John 20:22-3). But their real consecration was accomplished by the descent of the Holy Spirit in the shape of tongues of fire, which "rested on each one of them" (Acts 2:3).

In the Apostles Our Lord laid the foundation of the hierarchy; to deny this would be to oppose the will of the Lord. Of course the Apostles, by their consecration, did not become equal to or like Our Lord, vicars of Christ, or substitutes for Christ, neither in the person of St. Peter, nor in the persons of the Twelve taken collectively. Our Lord Himself lives invisibly in the Church, as its head; since His Ascension, He lives in the Church "always, now and forever and to eternity." The hierarchy of the Apostles did not receive the power to become vicars of Christ, but that of communicating the gifts necessary to the life of the Church. In other words, the apostolic hierarchy was instituted by the power and the will of Christ, but neither in the person of a prime hierarch (the Pope), nor in that of the entire apostolic assembly, does it take the place of Christ on earth. To the hierarchy belongs the authority to be mediators, servants of Christ, from whom they received full power for their ministry.

This ministry consists above all in preaching ''as eye-witnesses of the Word,'' ''as witnesses'' (Acts 1:8) of the Incarnation, in conferring the gifts of the Holy Spirit on the newly baptized, and in ordaining others to perform priestly functions, whatever they may be. In a word, the Apostles were given power to organize the life of the Church, and at the same time they were charismatics who united in themselves the gift of the administration of the sacraments with those of prophecy and of teaching. Associated with the Twelve were other Apostles, not of the same dignity—as it were, inferior. These were the 70 Apostles or disciples spoken of in the Gospel, and the Apostles (other than the Twelve) mentioned in the apostolic epistles. First place here belongs certainly to St. Paul, whose superior dignity, equal to that of the original group, is testified to by himself and recognized by the others. To this same group belong, further, all those who saw the risen Lord (1 Cor. 15:5-8), for example, Barnabas, Silas, Timothy, Apollos, Andronicus, and Junius. But this apostolate (see the ''Didache'' document at the end of the first century) differed essentially from the proto-apostolate, the apostolate of the Twelve, who possessed the plenitude of gifts, who were invested with full power by Christ, and sent by Him to ''bear witness.''

These twelve Apostles, called by Our Lord, died before the end of the first century. In the East, there remained only the ''elder'' John, who outlived all the others. Did the power of the apostolic ministry in the Church end after the death of the Apostles? In a certain sense, it did. It ended after its mission was accomplished, after having laid the foundation for the Church of the New Covenant and having preached the Gospel to all the world. The apostolate in the plenitude of its spiritual gifts has not and cannot have personal continuity, and the Roman idea that the Apostle Peter continues to exist, in the person of the Pope, is a willful dogmatic invention, incapable of logical confirmation. The apostolic gifts and powers were personal; Our Lord gave them to the Apostles in calling them by name. Besides, the apostolate is a synthesis of different charismatic gifts, a synthesis which we do not find in any of the hieratic powers of their followers in the apostolic succession. Nevertheless, the Apostles did not leave the world without bequeathing a heritage, a continuation of their ministry. The Apostles transmitted what they could transmit and what could be received by others. Outside the personal apostolic dignity, which could not be transmitted, they gave those gifts which belong either to Christians individually or to the Church as a society. They gave to all believers the gifts of grace of the Holy Spirit, which, conferred by the laying-on of hands, make those believers an elect body, a royal priesthood, a "holy" nation (1 Peter 2:9), but they agreed that these gifts should be communicated by means of a hierarchy instituted by them, whose authority exists by virtue of direct and uninterrupted succession from the Apostles.

After the Apostles, the communication of the gifts of the Holy Spirit in the Church became the prerogative of the hierarchy, that is of the episcopate, with its presbyters and deacons. Beginning from the end of the first and the outset of the second centuries, in the works of St. Ignatius, of St. Ireneus of Lyon, of Tertullian, and later, in the third century, in the works of St. Cyprian, the idea is developed that the Church is centered about the bishop, and that the bishop exists by virtue of the apostolic succession, which is a divine institution. In certain cases, examples are indicated of that succession uninterrupted (as in the sees of Rome, of Ephesus, of Jerusalem). It is impossible to state, historically, the place, the time and the manner of the institution by the Apostles of the hierarchy in its present form, that is in the three orders: bishops, presbyters, deacons. The documents of the beginning of the first century are silent on this point. Or indeed, if we find suggestions about the hieratic dignities it is evident that the orders there have another meaning than that of our day, or that the distinction and the correlation between the three degrees, very clear today, at that time lacked precision (Acts 20:17,28; Titus 1:5-7; 1 Tim. 2,5,7; 1 Peter 5:1-5). In any case, if we find in the writings of the Apostles indications about bishops and presbyters, these indications cannot be considered direct proofs of the existence of the three degrees of priesthood in the sense we give them now.

To prove that in the first century there existed a hierarchy with three orders, in the sense accepted today, is hardly possible and scarcely necessary. The picture given in 1 Cor. 12:14 corresponds rather with a life not yet well organized, but rich in inspiration and characterized by a diffusion of spiritual gifts. The charismatics naturally found leadership and direction in the Apostles. Doubtless also the Apostles instituted, by the laying-on of hands, leaders among the groups, who were named bishops or presbyters, or angels of the Church (Apocalypse), not to mention the ministry of deacons. What is indisputable is the presence of the hierarchy about the Apostles, by the side of the Apostles, it cannot be admitted that the formation of that hierarchy is the result only of a "natural" development of communal organization and that it was not also the realization of the direct will of Our Lord. In this connection we note that in Asia Minor (Epistle of St. Ignatius) and in Rome (Epistles of Pope Clement, work of St. Ireneus) towards the beginning of the second century, there existed a "monarchical" episcopate, that is, local churches having as heads bishops, as sole true charismatics, about whom presbyters and deacons are gathered. At that period the dogmatic expression of this system is still unstable, intermittent and often partial and exaggerated (as in the epistle of St. Ignatius of Antioch), but the custom, as well as the consciousness of it, is already present.

This transition from an unordered general "charismatism" to a closed clergy with an episcopate at its head remains a puzzle for the historian. It is sometimes understood by Protestants to have been a sort of spiritual catastrophe or general falling into sin, as a result of which amorphous communities everywhere became infected with institutionalism, adopted the forms of the organization of the state, and thus gave rise to "ecclesiastical law." This is an instance of the lack of feeling, so characteristic of Protestantism, for the oneness of the Church and its tradition, because of which much apparent difficulty and uncertainty arise. This leads to the idea that inwardly there is a break between the first and second centuries, an idea which leads to an absurdity—namely, that the Church could continue its existence in the true sense, free from hierarchical organization, only a few decades, after which the Church suddenly became afflicted with the hierarchic leprosy, and for 1,500 years ceased to be itself, until, suddenly, the Church was healed of this ailment and again became sound in anti-hierarchical Protestantism.

The hierarchy, in episcopal form, with presbyters and deacons dependent on it, responds to a natural necessity in the Church. Nothing is more natural than the need for such a hierarchy. The grace of the Holy Spirit given to the Church is not a personal, subjective inspiration of one or another person, which may exist or not; it is rather an objective fact in the life of the Church, the power of a universal Pentecost continuously active. The tongues of fire of Pentecost, sent down on the Apostles, live in the world and are communicated by the Apostles, who received them, to their successors. The assembly of the Apostles was the hieratic receptacle and the tongues of fire, the method of transmission of the gifts of grace of the Church. In view of this, the charismatic succession of the Apostles became necessary and inevitable. But this had to happen in a well-defined manner, valid for all, and not accidental, that is, by the regular succession of the hierarch, which—to put it in terms of sacramental theology—must operate not ''opere operantis'' but ''opere operato.'' A form for this succession prepared and instituted by God, was in existence: that of the priest of Old Testament, which according to the Epistle to the Hebrews, was the prototype of the priesthood of the New Testament. Nevertheless, this latter was not simply a continuation of the old. It was a new creation proceeding from the great High Priest, not after the order of Aaron, but after that of Melchizedek. This High Priest is Our Lord Jesus Christ, Who sacrifices to the Father not the blood of lambs, but His own blood, at once the priest and the sacrifice. The presence of Christ on earth naturally rendered superfluous and impossible the existence of a hierarchy outside Himself, but the formation of a hierarchy is also impossible without Our Lord, without His command. And the Apostles, as proto-hierarchs, transmitted to their successors their hieratic powers, but not their personal gifts in full plenitude. They communicated such powers as were of a general character.

We cannot affirm that the Apostles instituted this succession immediately, but the fact of such institution cannot be denied. After some fluctuation the hierarchy was formed in the second century after the type of the priesthood of the Old Testament, yet always with a difference, For the Church, which lives in the unity of tradition, the institution of the apostolic succession of the hierarchy is axiomatic. Tradition remains the same, always possessed of the same power, whether a certain form or institution appears in the first or the second or the twentieth century, if only the new form contains, not a denial, but a completion of what has previously been contained in the substance of tradition. The destruction or the denial of the content of tradition of the whole Church is a break and a spiritual catastrophe which impoverishes and deforms the life of the Church by taking from it the fullness of its inheritance.

Such is the effect of the abolition of the apostolic succession in Protestantism. It has deprived the Protestant world of the gifts of Pentecost, transmitted in the Sacraments and the cult of the Church by the hierarchy, which received its power from the Apostles and their successors. The Protestant world thus became like Christians who, although baptized ''in the name of the Lord Jesus,'' have not received the Holy Spirit transmitted by the hands of the Apostles (Acts 19:5-6). Certainly God ''gives not the spirit by measure,'' and those who are baptized with the baptism of Christ in the name of the Holy Trinity already have the assurance of the Holy Spirit, which ''blows where it wills.'' The possibility of immediate and direct action of the Holy Spirit on man by the power of a new Pentecost, or even of a prolonged Pentecost, cannot be completely excluded. But it can be stated that ''no one knows whence the spirit comes and whither it goes,'' while Christ, by His will, has established in His Church definite and recognized modes for the reception of the Holy Spirit—as in the case cited above, when the Apostles, by the laying-on of hands, transmitted it. These modes are the sacraments of the Church administered by a priest of the apostolic succession.

The fact of this succession, and the continuity of the laying-on of hands, which cannot be disputed, especially from the beginning of the second century, is in itself sufficient evidence of its divine institution. This applies equally to the Eastern and the Western Churches. Of course, this laying-on of hands is not to be conceived as some form of magic, and the priesthood is valid only in union with the Church. Be it noted, in the Church, not above the Church or outside it, in either of which cases its validity is lost.

The denial of a hierarchical succession in Protestantism, is based on the idea of a universal priesthood and communal election. But the fact that all Christians possess grace, and that in this sense a universal priesthood exists, in no way contradicts the existence of a special priesthood, the hierarchy. The universal priesthood is not only compatible with the hierarchy, but is even a condition of the existence of the latter. For certainly the hierarchy cannot come into being and continue in a society deprived of grace; on the contrary, in such societies the hierarchy loses its power, as is the case in groups becoming entirely heretical or schismatic. But both gifts and ministries vary. While there may be different degrees of priesthood in the limits of the same hierarchy, there can and there ought to be a difference between the hierarchy and the laity, even granted a universal priesthood. It is equally a mistake to place opposite each other election by the group and the laying-on of hands, as if the latter could replace or exclude the former. On the contrary, election by communal choice, while a preliminary condition, is entirely compatible with the decisive value of the laying-on of hands. Human will and choice cannot alone take the place of the divine act of imposition. And the officer elected by the group does not by that election become either a hierarch or a charismatic. The hierarchy is the only charismatic ministry of the Church having permanent value; it takes the place of a vanished special "charismatism." Generally speaking, this is the explanation of the historic fact that the unregulated charismatism of the primitive Church was replaced, in the time of the Apostles, by regular charismatism and by the apostolic succession.

The hierarchy must be understood as a regular, legal charismatism for a special purpose. Partly for the mystical transmission of the gifts of grace and, the succession of life in grace. As a result of this regulation, bound up with the external fact of the hierarchical succession, the hierarchy, not losing its charismatism, becomes an institution, and thus into the life of the Church is introduced institutionalism or canonical law. But this institutionalism is of a very special nature, of which we must here take account.

Above all, and this is the most essential thing, the hierarchy is the power for administering the sacraments; consequently the hierarchy carries in itself that mysterious power, superhuman and supernatural. According to the testimony of ancient writings (Apostolic Fathers such as St. Ignatius of Antioch) the bishop is he who celebrates the Eucharist, and only the Eucharist celebrated by a bishop is valid. The sacrament of the breaking of bread occupied at once the most important place in the Christian life; it became the organizing force in the Church and especially for the hierarchy. After Pentecost, the believers ''devoted themselves to the Apostles' teaching and fellowship, to the breaking of bread and the prayers'' (Acts 2:42). The central significance of the Eucharist in the life of the Church is attested by many documents of the first and second centuries. It was natural that, at first, the Eucharist should be celebrated by the Apostles, also by the charismatics (Didache) instituted by the Apostles. But in post-apostolic times the administration of the sacrament of the Body and Blood fell to bishops alone. Little by little, in the usage of the Church, other sacraments were joined to the first. Then the hierarchy, that is the bishops and the clergy dependent on them, immediately joined together for the administering of the sacraments as a consequence of the sacramental ''charismatism.'' This latter, being the foundation of the mystic life, of the life of grace in the Church, had to have permanent representatives. The bishop, possessed of the fullness of charismatic power, naturally and inevitably became the center around whom revolved all the ecclesiastical community, which depended essentially upon him.

It is thus easy to understand the logic of Christian thought of the first centuries, from St. Ignatius to St. Cyprian. According to them, "episcopum in ecclesia esse et ecclesiam in episcopo." From this general charismatic foundation there came, later in the history of the Church, the development of canonical law which defined the rights of the bishops in the Church, and still later the relations among the bishops. In the course of the centuries, local and ecumenical councils regulated these mutual relations, which, even now, give evidence of the complexity of the situation at that time. The essential point is that the bishops, notwithstanding canonical differences due to historic circumstances, are entirely equal from the charismatic viewpoint: among them there never was a super-bishop, "episcopus episcoporum," never a pope.

To appreciate properly the nature of the episcopal authority we must bear in mind its special features, arising from the nature of communion in the Church. It must be noted that in spite of its being often labelled "monarchical," the authority of the Church is of quite a different nature from that of the state. It is a spiritual authority, which is above all a form of service (Luke 22:26). In the use of his power the bishop works within the Church, but never above the Church, which is a spiritual organism, one of love. Agreement with the Church, and union with it, is the very condition of the existence of the bishop. This union cannot be expressed in terms of constitutional right, such as those of democracy or of limited monarchical power, because these categories of right are not applicable here. If the Church law has authority at all, it is always an authority sui generis. The episcopal power may be even more absolute than that of an absolute monarch but still remains entirely latent and diffused in the union of the bishop and his people.

The example of the Church in Jerusalem, in its relations with the Apostles, as the first bishops, serves as a guiding rule in this connection. Notwithstanding all the plenitude of their power, really "super-episcopal" (for over and above the plenitude of episcopal power they had also full apostolic authority personally), the Apostles decided all essential questions in union with the people (see Acts 1:15-16; 23-24, 26; 6:2-6; 11:23; 15:6, 25). And if history tells us that the ecumenical as well as many local councils were usually composed of bishops alone, this fact should not be interpreted as a new canon law abrogating the council of the Apostles and giving to the rank of bishop, as such, power over the people of the Church, valid without their participation. The fact must be understood not as an expression of the power of the bishops over the Church, but rather as a representation by the bishops of the churches of which they are the heads and with which they remain united. That the ''elders and the brothers'' of the council of Jerusalem were not actually present at all subsequent councils was the result of practical considerations or technical convenience. As a matter of fact, the All-Russian Council in Moscow, 1917-18, consisted of diocesan bishops, together with their flocks, priests and laymen. Thus organized, the council of Moscow followed more exactly than the ecumenical councils the canon law of Jerusalem. The difficulties of travel, due to contemporary means of communication, sufficiently explained the solely hierarchic composition of the councils. It may also be held that the people of the Church were represented by the Emperor and his functionaries.

It is true that in Roman Catholicism the presence of bishops alone has become a general rule, for the hierarchy has been understood rather as authority over the Church, a power of which the Pope-monarch is the head. But we do not know, in the history of apostolic times, one single instance of the Apostles having acted as a personal authority over the Church, independent of it. As to the personal gifts of the Apostles—for example, that of performing miracles—these were not allied to their prerogatives as representatives of ecclesiastical power, but belonged to them as one of the ''gifts'' of their apostolic ministry. This is why, up to the present time, the people of the Church have the right to a voice in the choice of bishops; the people join even in ordination, when performed by bishops, for, at a certain moment, the people must announce if the elect is worthy—axios—or unworthy. "Let no one be ordained," wrote Pope Leo the Great, "contrary to the consent and will of the people, for fear lest the people, having been forced, begin to hate and to despise the undesirable bishop" (Epist. ad Anast. 84).

To understand thoroughly the hieratic principle of the Church, we must think not only of the unquestionable prerogatives of the hierarchy, but also of those, no less unquestionable, of the laity. The laity are not merely passive subjects with their only obligation that of obeying the hierarchy; they are not in any way vessels empty of "charism" to be filled by the hierarchy. The lay state should be considered as a sacred dignity; the name Christian has made "a people of God, a royal priesthood." The significance of this idea, although it is sometimes exaggerated in Protestantism, even to the complete denial of the hierarchy, must never be minimized. As a Christian having received baptism and the gift of the Holy Spirit through anointing, which may be conceived as a sort of ordination to the calling of Christian, the laity is also charismatic, though in a limited sense, especially in connection with the celebration of the liturgy and the administration of the sacraments. They can, in case of need, administer baptism. In the sacraments whose administration is reserved to priests alone, particularly the Eucharist, even here the laity have a certain share; the priest, strictly speaking, cannot complete the sacrament alone, without the people. In other words, he administers the sacraments with the people, and the laity are co-administrators with him. In the spiritual organism which is the Church everything takes place in the unity of love, and not one organ can exist without the others. "Nonne et laici sacerdotes sumus?" Up to a certain point the words of Tertullian are applicable here.

The New Testament has no direct instances of the hierarchy in its now accepted three degrees, deacons, priests and bishops; on the other hand there is no evidence of a completely unorganized administration of the sacraments. This function seems always to belong either to the Apostles or to other individuals specially appointed. The hierarchy, in direct succession from the Apostles, and the One Who appointed them, is Christ Himself, acting in the Church. There can be no greater misfortune in the Church than that great movement beginning in the sixteenth century, by which whole congregations, whole nations, deprived themselves of the hierarchy. Of course "the Spirit goes where it wills," and it is impossible to say that these churches are altogether deprived of the Holy Spirit, Nevertheless, this is one of the deepest sorrows of the Christian Church today, and we must all pray for a time when our Protestant brothers should again seek and again receive a hierarchy. Protestants sometimes find an opposition between prophecy and institutionalism. They think that the hieratic principle is antagonistic to the gift of prophecy which abounds in the church when the hierarchy is eliminated. This opposition, which is justified in a certain degree by the excess of Romanism, rests on a fundamental misunderstanding. In the beginning, at the time of the Apostles and in the primitive Church, different gifts existed, among them that of prophecy. St. Paul encouraged this: "I want you...to prophesy"; "Earnestly desire to prophesy" (1 Cor. 14:5, 39). On the one hand the Apostle wished to safeguard prophecy for fear it would be extinguished ("Quench not the spirit, despise not prophecy"), but at the same time, he develops the idea of a body with divers members. And although prophecy was widespread in the Church in apostolic times, it was not opposed to the "institutionalism" of the episcopate, the presbyteriate and the diaconate, which we find existing in the apostolic epistles and even in the Acts.

The hieratic principle has as much value for the Church as that of prophecy, if the latter is understood as a generalized inspiration. The acquisition of the gifts of the Holy Spirit is the end of the Christian life, according to the definition of St. Seraphim, the greatest Russian saint of the nineteenth century, The first Christian preaching of St. Peter contained the prophetic words of Joel, applied to the Christian Church: "I will fill with my spirit every creature, your sons and your daughters shall prophesy" (Acts 2:17), and that Pentecostal word is always to be heard in the Church. The Orthodox Church repeats here the words of Moses: "Would that all Jehovah's people were prophets" (Num. 11:29). But this idea of general prophecy, the aquisition of the Holy Spirit, which the Church encourages, may become an illusory pretension when it denies the hierarchy in the name of a universal priesthood; prophecy then transforms itself into a pseudo-prophetic excitement. This latter was overcome in the Church in "Montanism," and the Church continues to prevail over all such successive heresies. Such an error leads, besides, to a ritual officialdom, devoid of grace, as in the case of ministers elected but not consecrated, who claim to replace the divinely instituted hierarchy. They pretend to concentrate in themselves the general gift of prophecy, thus depriving their flock of it. Is not this "institutionalism," bureaucratic instead of hieratic, when the latter is eliminated by the former?

The priestly service, as a charismatic mediation, cannot be merely mechanical or magical: it presupposes the spiritual participation of the person who serves as a living mediator. In acting as mediator between God and man in the sacrament, in causing the descent of the Holy Spirit, the priest makes himself the instrument of that descent; he renounces his own individuality, he dies with the victim, he is at the same time sacrificed and sacrificer, "he who offers and that which is offered" in the image of Christ, the High Priest. This death is love's renunciation of self; the minister of the hierarchy is the minister of love. The connection between the clergy and the laity does not consist in the authority of the former over the latter, but in their mutual love. The pastors receive the special gift of compassionate love. The sufferings and the faults of others become theirs. They care for souls in applying to them acts of love and of pardon, as well as the corrections of discipline. The clergy are charged with a special responsibility toward their flocks, a responsibility nonexistent for the laity; the latter repay their pastors by loving and honoring them. The flock groups itself naturally around the shepherds, and the Church is thus composed of hieratically organized communities.

The hierarchy is a sort of skeleton of the body of the Church. Certainly if at any time there appears in the Church a manifestation of the spirit and its power—through any man whatsoever—all ecclesiastical society relates itself to this "prophetic" minister; pastors and flocks, regardless of hieratic difference, follow the prophet. The personal authority of St. Seraphim of Sarov, or of Father John of Kronstadt, or of the "startsi" (elders) of the monastery of Optina (Fr. Ambrose and others), was greater than that of any hierarch. But this authority never encroached upon the prerogatives of the hierarchy. It kept within its limitations and by no means abolished them. This fact confirms once more the compatibility between prophecy and hierarchy.

The duties of the shepherd include the duty of instruction in the Church. This duty is joined so naturally to the priesthood that it would seem strange to have it otherwise. Not only the reading but also the preaching of the word of God, by direct instruction, form part of the pastoral ministry. The words of the pastor, independent of their greater or lesser value, have an importance deriving from the place and time where they are spoken, for they form a part of the divine service. In this role of doctor of the Church the pastor can neither be replaced nor supplanted.

But the duties of the doctor are not limited to preaching in the temple. Hence the right and the duty of the hierarchy to preserve intact the teaching transmitted by the Church, protecting it from deformation and announcing to believers the basis of true doctrine. The maintenance of this basis is assured by various appropriate measures belonging to the ecclesiastical calling, even to excommunication. Within the limits of his diocese, the bishop guards the purity of the doctrines taught and pronounced; the council of bishops of a regional Church, or even, in cases of more general importance, the council of bishops of the ecumenical Church, define ecclesiastical truth which has been obscured or has never been made clear in the mind of the Church.

If it is remembered that priests must not only preach in the temple but teach elsewhere, then the general question arises concerning the nature of that teaching, in so far as it belongs to the hierarchy alone. Here enters the question of infallibility. In the Church there are shepherds and the flock; there are then two parts, those who teach and those who are taught. The teaching authority of the Church cannot be diminished with impunity. But this does not at all mean that all teaching belongs to the pastors and that the laity are entirely without this function, having only the duty of passive acceptance of doctrines taught. Such a point of view, which sharply divides ecclesiastical society into two parts, the active and the passive, does not agree with the true inwardness of Christianity, and, together with the Protestants, we must contrast this idea with that of the universal priesthood, of the anointing of the people of God. It is to the people, to all believers, to all Christianity and not the hierarchy alone (as ultra-hieratists believe) that the words of Our Saviour were addressed: ''Go then, teach all nations,'' and again: ''Go into all the world and preach the Gospel to the whole creation'' (Mark 16:15).

If the administration of the sacraments, if especially the laying-on of hands was the prerogative of the Apostles (and later of the hierarchy instituted by them), the preaching of the Gospel was to an equal degree considered the work of all believers. For every believer is called by Our Lord Himself to confess (and thus to preach) before men (Matt. 10:32-3; Luke 18:9). And truly we see that the preaching of Christ was the work, from the beginning, not only of the Apostles, but of believers in general (Acts 6:5; 8:5, 12, 14, 26-36); and not only by men, but also by women of whom some were glorified by the Church as equal to the Apostles because of their preaching of the Gospel (St. Nina, apostle of Georgia, St. Mary Magdalene, St. Thecla the Martyr, and others). The Christian mission is not limited to the hierarchy, but is the duty of each Christian, who says ''I believe and I confess,'' and who, in so doing, becomes a preacher. The great deeds of the martyrs, who confessed their faith, are the best sermons.

Further, if we consider preaching, not only among unbelievers but among Christians, we find in Scripture numerous witnesses to the active role of the laity. Note also that the Scriptures do not know the word "laity," but that the New Testament calls Christians simply "believers," "disciples," "brothers," etc. The laity then share in the gift of teaching, thus proving the existence of a special gift of teaching (James 5:19-20; 1 Thess. 5:11; Hebrews 3:13; Gal. 6:1; 1 Cor. 14:26; Col. 3:16; 1 Tim. 1:7, 3:2, 5:17; 1 Peter 4:10-11). But if the laity have not the right to preach during services (as they have not the power to celebrate the mysteries during which the word is preached) they are not deprived of the right to preach apart from the service, and, still more, to preach outside the temple. A certain limitation of the right of the laity to preach was introduced for practical and disciplinary reasons, but not at all because of charismatic inferiority, or of the incompatibility of the right of preaching with the status of the laity. In the Church there is no place for speechlessness and for blind obedience, as the Apostle says in Gal. 5:1.

But if this is true of the work of edification in the Church, still less can the laity be denied the right to scientific study of doctrinal problems, or even to be theologians. At all events, in our day, by the very force of circumstance, such occupation is equivalent to teaching. The exercise of this right may be regulated by the hierarchy, but not abolished. Theological thought is the conscience of the Church; it is its very breath of life which cannot be controlled externally. Besides the general grace given to Christians by the Holy Spirit, there can be a special election, formerly termed the prophetic ministry, which must not be overlooked. Because of a certain timidity and the difficulty of recognizing this election, it is seldom actually designated as prophecy; but certainly the springs of this gift in the Church have not dried up.

In our time the terms "prophet" and "prophecy" have become rather literary epithets. But these words ought to express our religious conviction that prophecy has not ceased and cannot cease in the Church. The Apostle expressly forbade the scorning of prophecies and the extinction of the spirit (1 Thess. 5:19-20). But the spirit blows where it wills; the gift of prophecy by the Holy Spirit is not connected with the hieratic ministry, though it may be united

with it. It is true that discrimination between spirits and the
recognition of authentic prophecy are an extremely difficult task for
the Church, for there is always the danger of error. Hence the
Apostle says: ''Test everything; hold fast what is good'' (1 Thess.
5:21). Nevertheless he himself warns us not to quench the spirit.
Such an extinction would occur if the laity were formally forbidden
to be free theologians. To be sincere one must be free; freedom does
not mean ''free thought'' but freedom of thought; it is neither simple ignorance of traditional ecclesiastical doctrine nor license.
Freedom is a true and personal inspiration, penetration into the
depth of what is crystallized in the Church, a desire to make real the
experience of the Church in the realm of personal feeling and
thought. This latter corresponds with fundamental reality, for the
tradition of the Church is also personal experience realized as individuals. This domain of free inspiration in the Church, and also
that of scientific study, is preferably the domain of ''prophecy'' in
the sense which it is understood today. But this domain cannot be
the exclusive privilege of the hierarchy. It belongs to the entire
Christian world.

Of The Infallible Exterior
Authority Of The Church

Does any member of the Church possess of himself personal infallibility in his judgment of dogma? No, he does not. Even Catholic
doctrine does not ascribe to the Pope a personal infallibility, but only when he speaks ''ex cathedra.'' Every member of the Church is
liable to error, or rather to the introduction of his own limitations,
in his personal dogmatic study. The history of the Church bears
witness in this regard that no hieratic position, however exalted,
secures one against the danger of error. There were heretic popes
(Liberius and Honorius), not to mention the frequent divergencies
of ideas between certain popes, implying certainly that one or the
other was wrong. There have been patriarchs (of Constantinople
and Alexandria), bishops, priests and laity, all heretical. No one can

pretend to personal infallibility in theological matters, and such infallibility attaches to no single office. This holds for all hierarchs taken separately, and all the more for the hierarchy as a whole.

The ecclesiastical authors, St. Ignatius of Antioch, St. Ireneus, St. Cyprian, admonish believers to gather around their bishops, and the teaching of the bishop is considered the norm of the truth of the Church, the criterion of tradition. This special authority of judgment, allied to his office, belongs to a bishop as such, and even more rightly to the head of a particular Church, joined with him in unity of life and grace, of love and thought. The bishop who confesses the faith, in the name of his Church and as its mouthpiece, is joined with it in union of love and in conformity of thought, in the spirit of the words preceding the recitation of the creed in the Orthodox liturgy: ''Let us love one another that we may with one mind confess . . .'' In other words, the right to voice the doctrine of the Church belongs to the bishop, as someone not above but in the community of which he is the head. In the same way the assembly of bishops, the episcopate of a church ecumenical or local, united in special council, or living in union and in connection, either by correspondence or by means of intermediaries, does not possess the necessary supreme authority to expound doctrine except in union with the Church and in harmony with it. The episcopate neither legislates for, nor commands the Church independently of that organization, but is its specially endowed representative. The authority of the bishop is fundamentally the authority of the Church; as the latter is constituted hierarchically it expresses itself by the mouth of the episcopate.

Since the episcopate is the final authority for the administration of the sacraments, it is clear that their doctrinal decisions have the same sacramental authority. These decisions are canons or ecclesiastical laws which must be obeyed, since the Church must be obeyed. Thus it follows that the hierarchy, represented by the episcopate, becomes a sort of external doctrinal authority which regulates and normalizes the dogmatic life of the Church. Certainly such doctrinal definitions by one hierarch or by the whole episcopate invested with ecclesiastical authority and rendered ''ex cathedra'' in the carrying out of the episcopal ministry, must be carefully distinguished from personal theological opinions of the same bishop or bishops, considered simply as private theologians or authors. These private opinions are by no means obligatory for their flocks. These opinions vary with the personal capacities of their authors. Only those acts done in accordance with the pastoral ministry have the force of law for the flock.

Inasmuch as the Church is a unity of faith and belief, bound together by the hierarchic succession, it must have its doctrinal definitions supported by the whole authority of the Church. In the process of determining these truths the episcopate gets together with the laity, and appears as representative of the latter. From this the bishops derive the authority to announce doctrinal truths and demand adherence to them.

A moment may arrive in the life of the Church when the episcopate feels the authority to pronounce the truth in the name of the Church, to be the mouthpiece of the Church. From this it is only one step to the conclusion of the Vatican Council by which, in virtue of the gift of pronouncing the truth which belongs to the Church (charisma veritatis), infallibility (ex cathedra) belongs to the bishop. Let us leave aside for the moment the question as to whether individual or collective authority is concerned. Here arises a problem relating to the external infallible spokesman of the doctrine of the Church. Does such an agency exist? Is it indispensable? Is it possible in the Church?

At first sight it seems that life and doctrine give a positive response to these questions. An episcopal authority exists, whose aim is to safeguard doctrinal purity; that is incontestable. This authority is necessary to the Church, as a security against personal, anarchical thought destructive of unity. The existence of such an agency is possible, for, in fact, it has been manifested and continues to manifest itself in the Church. It is however necessary to define and limit this authority.

The hierarchy, by its authority, protects the doctrine already accepted by the Church, the ecclesiastical tradition; it takes care to decide if new doctrinal definitions can become effective parts of that tradition. The first point raises no doubts: it is natural that the "depositum fidei," that is, all which the Church already possesses, should be protected by the hieratic power although this "depositum fidei" is contained by the whole Church. The other question is, in principle, much more difficult. New doctrinal decisions, once admitted, come under the protection of the hierarchy. But, if they are promulgated by that same hierarchy, whence comes their force, whence do they receive the sanction of their verity: from that same hierarchy or from the whole Church? In the first case, all power to guard and to define truth would belong to the hierarchy, which could thus command the Church by virtue of its "charisma veritatis." Thus the Church would be considered as divided into two parts: those who teach and those who are taught; on the one hand, the episcopate with the clergy; on the other, the laity. There would exist neither judgment, thought, opinion nor tradition of the Church, for all these would belong to the hierarchy. For the flock there remains only one duty, that of obedience, which Catholic theology calls (not without a sort of irony) "infallibilitas passiva." All power to judge, "infallibilitas activa," thus reverts to the hierarchy, possessor of a special "charisma veritatis." The term veritas receives an abstract and theoretical meaning. It is not true life in the Church, equally inherent in all, but an abstract knowledge, reserved solely for the elect (the hierarchy) and communicated or not by these elect to the ignorant. But Christ is the truth, life in the Church, in the body of Christ is the truth; it is life in the truth, the true life, which possesses real knowledge and the power to express itself. In distinguishing "infallibilitas activa" from "infallibilitas passiva," that is to say, in admitting that the truth is known only to the hierarchy, a special esoterism is introduced into the idea of the Church. There would be initiates, possessing gnosis, and non-initiates, lacking it themselves, but capable of receiving it from the hierarchy. The Christian conception of hierarchy is thus replaced by a gnostic conception. The "charisma veritatis" is certainly inherent in the Church which is "the pillar and the bulwork of the Truth." But, according to the foregoing theory, the charisma becomes the portion, not of the whole body of the Church, but of the hierarchy only.

These ideas are developed with the greatest consistency in the Roman system and have become fixed in the Vatican dogma. The Pope possesses in himself all the fullness of "charisma veritatis" inherent in the Church; consequently he has the power to proclaim the truth infallibly, in the name of the Church, "ex cathedra," and this is exclusively of his own personal knowledge and not from the collective knowledge of the Church. The Pope not only proclaims the truth held by the Church, he not only commands, as supreme representative of the hierarchy, faithfulness to that truth, but he testifies himself to that truth, he possesses it, he discovers it for the Church.

Thus truth is held to be a sort of external knowledge belonging only to one person, and communicated by him to others. Here we have a clear division of the Church into the teachers and the taught, which is directly opposed to the words of the Saviour to His disciples, among whom was Peter. "But you are not to be called rabbi, for you have one teacher, . . . the Christ" (Matt. 23:8,10). The ministry of one person is here manifested, although it would be very difficult to decide when he speaks "ex cathedra." Everything becomes less clear when the papal function is attributed to a council of bishops, to an episcopal college, as was the case at the time of the councils of the Catholic reformers of Constance and Basle. A full agreement in thought, equivalent to a papal decision, would be possible only by the unanimity of all the episcopate, but this does not appear, even in the time of the ecumenical councils, and would be, for whatever cause, something quite exceptional. Lacking that unanimity, the voice of truth is expressed by the majority, that is according to the parliamentary system, with all its problems of the size of a given majority, and so on.

But whatever the organ of ecclesiastical infallibility which an nounces dogmatic truth to the Church, whether it be individual or

collective, it equally deprives the Church of the general gift of
teaching and of integral infallibility. Our Lord spoke only of Himself
as pastor of the sheep and He charged Peter to feed His sheep. This
means that the Church, the body of Christ, has Christ at its head.
He is the Truth, and the Church is the support of the Truth. In
relation to Him, the Church can have only a passive being, the
"flock of Christ." It is vain for the bishop of Rome, or for a council
of bishops, to attribute to themselves the power of Christ over the
Church. As successor of the Apostles, the Pope (or a group playing
the same role) wishes to be the vicar of Christ on earth, but Christ
left no vicar after Him. He lives, Himself, in the Church, "now,
always and forever." The Church is infallible as such, in its being as
a Church. Each member of the Church, inasmuch as he shares in
the life of the Church, lives in the truth; this is why infallibility
belongs to the whole Church. "With us the guardian of piety is the
very body of the Church, that is, the people themselves, who will
always preserve their faith unchanged" (Epistle of the Eastern
Patriarchs, 1849).

It is unthinkable that the mind of the Church, its very conscience, should belong to one only among its members, to a hierarchy placed above the body of the Church and announcing to it the
truth. A hierarchy placed above the people, that is, outside them,
separated from them, is no more capable of proclaiming the truth of
the Church than the people separated from the hierarchy, or than a
single isolated individual. In this separation from the Church and
this opposition to it the hierarchy would be outside the Church and
deprived of its spirit, for this spirit is union in love, and truth in the
Church is given only in the measure of that unity. The pretension
of the Pope to be the voice of the truth destroys the unity of the
Church; it puts the Pope in the place of the Church; "l'eglise c'est
moi."

The same is true of the hierarchy considered as the collective
episcopate. A guiding dogmatic principle is offered here by the
Jerusalem council of the Apostles from whom the hierarchy, in the
measure of their service, continue the succession. Strictly speaking,

the succession of gifts of the Holy Spirit, given to the Church at the time of Pentecost and descending by the Apostles and their followers, extends to the whole Church. The "apostolic succession," special and restricted, exists only for the sacramental ministry, for the priesthood and not for teaching and dogmatic consciousness. We see this exemplified in the Council of Jerusalem where there were assembled "the Apostles and with them the elders," that is, the older members of the community, people devoid of hieratic character. "Brethren, both the Apostles and the presbyters" (Acts 15:23), that is proto-hierarchs, the holy Apostles, in union with elders and brothers, decided and gave their pronouncements together. The fact is significant, for here is exemplified all the positive force of the unity of the Church, and, in accordance with that union, the assembly proclaimed: "It has seemed good to the Holy Spirit and to us" (Acts 15:28), in other words, to the Holy Spirit which lives in us by our union.

Hence the question of an exterior organ of infallibility in the Church by its very form faces us with heresy: the idea of the Church—a spiritual organism whose life is unity in love—is replaced by the principle of spiritual power. This is heresy.

Here we touch the very essence of the Orthodox doctrine of the Church. All the power of Orthodox ecclesiology is concentrated on this point. Without understanding this question it is impossible to understand Orthodoxy; it becomes an eclectic compromise, a middle way between the Roman and Protestant viewpoints. The soul of Orthodoxy is "sobornost" according to the perfect definition of Khomiakov: "in this one word there is contained a whole confession of faith." Russian ecclesiastical language and theology use this term in a large sense which no other language possesses; by it is expressed the power and the spirit of the Orthodox Church. What then is "sobornost"?

The word is derived from the verb "sobirat," to unite, to assemble. From this comes the word "sobor," which, by a remarkable coincidence, means both "council" and "church." Sobornost is the state of being together. The Slavonic text of the Nicene Creed translates the epithet "catholic," when applied to the Church, as "sobornaia," an adjective which may be understood in two ways, each equally exact. To believe in a "sobornaia" church is to believe in a Catholic Church, in the original sense of the word, in a Church that assembles and unites: it is also to believe in a conciliar Church in the sense Orthodoxy gives to the term, that is in a Church of the ecumenical councils, as opposed to a purely monarchical ecclesiology. To translate "sobornost," I have ventured to use the French word "conciliarite," "conciliarity," which must be used both in a restricted sense (the Church of the Councils) and in a larger sense (the Church Catholic, ecumenical). Sobornost may also be translated as "harmony," "unanimity." Orthodoxy, says Khomiakov, is opposed both to authoritarianism and to individualism; it is a unanimity, a synthesis of authority. It is the liberty in love, which unites believers. The word "sobornost" expresses all that.

This term evokes the ideas of catholicity and of ecumenicity, ideas connected but distinct. Ecumenicity means that the Church includes all peoples and all parts of the earth. Now this is the meaning that Roman Catholics generally give to the word "catholicity." A rather quantitative conception of catholicity (universal diffusion) has predominated in the West since Optat de Miletus (De Schism. donat II, 2) and especially since Augustine (De unit, eccles. 2). In the East, on the contrary, catholicity is understood in a sense rather qualitative (cf. Clement of Alexandria, Strom., 7:17., and above all St. Ignatius: "Where Jesus Christ is, there is the Catholic Church." Smyrn. 8). Catholicity or sobornost may be defined qualitatively. That corresponds to the true meaning of this concept in the history of philosophy, notably according to Aristotle, where "catholic" means, "that which is common," in contrast to "that which exists as a particular phenomenon." Here is a "Platonic" idea, according to Aristotle, an idea which exists, not at all above things, or, in a certain sense, before things (as in Plato), but in things, as their foundation and their truth. In this sense the Catholic Church means that which is in the truth, which shares the truth, which lives the true life. Then the definition "catholic," that is, "agreeing with all," "in entirety," shows in what this truth consists. It consists in the union of all the spirit of wisdom integral in the union of all.

In "sobornost" understood as "catholicity" each member of the Church, equally with the assembly of the members, lives in union with the entire Church, with the Church invisible, which is itself an uninterrupted union with the Church visible and forms its foundation. Then the idea of catholicity, in this sense, is turned inward and not outward. And each member of the Church is "Catholic" inasmuch as he is in union with the Church invisible, in the truth. Both the anchorite and those who live in the midst of the world, the elect who remain faithful to the truth in the midst of irreligion and general heresy, may be "Catholic." In this sense catholicity is the mystic and metaphysical depth of the Church and not at all its outward diffusion. Catholicity has neither external, geographical attributes, nor empirical manifestations. It is perceived by the spirit which lives in the Church and which searches our hearts. But it must be connected with the empirical world, with the Church visible. Catholicity is also conciliarity, in the sense of active reconciliation, of a participation in the integral life of the Church, in a life sharing the same truth.

But why is catholicity, in the sense of external ecumenicity, most often indicated as among the attributes of the true Church by the Fathers and Doctors, especially St. Cyprian and St. Augustine? They affirm that the Church is not limited to one place or one nation, but that it is everywhere and for all peoples; it is not the Church of a narrow circle or of a sect, but it is the Church of all humanity. There is a direct and positive relation between catholicity in the external sense and ecumenicity, the same relations as between the idea and the manifestation—noumenon and phenomenon. The things which are most profound and most interior are just those which belong to all men, for they reunite humanity, which, on the surface of empirical being, is divided. These things have a tendency to spread as fully and largely as possible, although this is hindered by opposing forces: sin, common to humanity, and temptation. Certainly, as both the words of Our Lord Himself and other escharological indications in the Bible tell us, only the elect will remain faithful in the latter days in the midst of temptations ("and if these days are not shortened, no creature will be saved").

There are, then, many positive reasons why the universal truth should become the truth for all, but because of negative factors opposing that universality the truth is realized only in limited fashion. Thus only a quantitative criterion of truth is insufficient, and the rule of Vincent of Lerins: "quod semper, quod ubique quod ab omnibus creditum est" is more an abstract principle than an historic reality; it is difficult to find a single epoch in the history of the Church when this principle is realized without limitations. To be specific: even in our day Orthodoxy does not possess a numerical majority in the Christian world; Catholicism, in spite of its external universality, cannot boast of a quantitative predominance. External ecumenicity also, while a natural and necessary manifestation of interior catholicity, is nevertheless not a primary but a derived characteristic. Ecumenicity, like the truth, like catholicity, is not dependent upon the quantitative, for "where two or three are gathered together in My name, there am I in the midst of them."

Integral conciliarity is not quantity but quality; it is participation in the Body of Christ, in which the Holy Spirit works. Life in Christ, by the Holy Spirit, is life in the truth, a life of unity, a life possessing wisdom and integrality, the spirit of integral wisdom. Divine Wisdom (Sophia) which is the Church existing in the spirit before time, constitutes the foundation and the source of catholicity. The truth of the Church is, above all, life in the truth, and not an abstract and theoretical knowledge. This life in the truth is accessible to man, not by opposition to the object of knowledge, but in union with it. It is never given to him in isolation or separated from other men, but in a union, living and immediate, in the unity of many in one whole (the image of the Holy Trinity, consubstantial and indivisible). The truth of the Church is given to the Church.

Here the words of Our Lord should be recalled: ''He who will save his soul must lose it.'' He who lives in union with others, who frees himself of the ''I,'' who renounces and leaves himself—he it is alone who can receive the truth. In giving up his individuality, the believer does not enter a metaphysical void, but a fullness. The Church, body of Christ, vivified by the Holy Spirit, is the supreme reality which we find in our being when we live in the Church. We learn to know that being when we leave our isolation; life in the Church is this ''conciliarity,'' by it we share in the true universal life of the body of Christ. Life in the Church understood as ''sobornost'' (''conciliarity'') is indefinable rationally, for it discloses itself only beyond the limits of rational thought. It is transcendent to the individual, while becoming immanent to him in the degree by which he is penetrated with the spirit of the Church; ''conciliarity'' is truth; truth is ''conciliarity.''

Such is the meaning of the ''infallibility'' of the Church. It is not the external certitude of assertion, as Roman Catholic theology thinks; that would be very little, for that is only an entirely negative property and limited to the domain of rational thought. Only an isolated assertion can be exact or inexact. It is, for example, exact that $2 \times 2 = 4$, but it is not exact that $2 \times 2 = 5$; it is exact that the Volga flows into the Caspian, but it is not exact that it flows into the Black Sea. The exactitude or inexactitude of an assertion treats in such instances only the validity, the reality of the connection established between subject and predicate. It is an entirely formal estimation of the assertion, not from the point of view of its content (subject and predicate), but from the point of view of the legitimacy of their union; in a strictly formal verification there is restraint, there is only ''yes'' and ''no,'' there is only affirmation and negation. Infallibility thus understood (and Catholic theology is very near to such a conception) in no way expresses the idea of the true Church. The Church is infallible, not because it expresses the truth correctly from the point of view of practical expediency, but because it contains the truth. The Church, truth, infallibility, these are synonymous.

Life in the Church, then, is life in the truth, and the truth is the spirit of the Church. In the place of truth we may say "conciliarity," for it is the same thing: to live in union with the Church is to live in the truth, and to live in the truth is to live in union with the Church. From the rational point of view this may appear a vicious circle. But the "vicious circle" in logical reason is a natural and necessary attribute of ontological assertion. To seek a criterion of the truth of the judgments of the Church, not in itself but outside it, would be to postulate the existence of a knowledge or a definition "supra-ecclesiastical," by the light of which the Church would understand its own spirit. Such an exterior definition of the Church does not and cannot exist. The Church knows itself directly.

This self-knowledge is the Church's infallibility. The Catholic attempt to find an external, ultra-ecclesiastical authority for infallibility in the Pope has been unsuccessful, because it has proved to be impossible to proclaim every personal decision of the Pope infallible, thus making the Pope and the Church absolutely equivalent. The Pope is held to be infallible only when he speaks "ex cathedra," that is in the spirit of the Church. But there is no definition of "ex cathedra" and there can be none. He speaks "ex cathedra" when he proclaims the truth, and he proclaims the truth when he speaks "ex cathedra." The "sobonost" of the Church, viewed in its relation to individual knowledge, corresponds to what is called subconscious and what should be called superconscious. In the life of the soul there are complexes which exist only in relation to "the union of many in one," but which are realized in individual psychology. These are the phenomena of collective psychology. These phenomena, however, concern chiefly the emotive and volitional life, while touching the super-individual domain. The true "conciliarity" of the Church is concerned above all with the spiritual life. It is the individual spirit merged into the unity of "many in one," it is the "I" grounded in the "we." In this plural unity of the Church—the body of Christ—lives the spirit of God. The opposite pole from "sobornost" understood as spiritual unity, is the spirit of the herd, taken as an emotional corporeal unity. The opposite pole from multi-unity in the Church, in which the personality attains its supreme actuality, is the collective, in which the personality, remaining within itself, enters into an agreement with others that is of an obligatory nature. In contrast a free union in love is the very essence of the spirit of the Church. In human life, this spiritual content is enclosed in a given frame, national, historical. But these different exteriors contain the same unique life in the Holy Spirit, and, in this sense, the Church is everywhere and in all times identical with itself and catholic. External ecumenicity is only an envelope showing forth the Church's essence and its constant identity. And it is only in an internal, not an external, sense, that the words of Vincent of Lerins may be accepted: ''quod semper, quod ubique, quod ab omnibus traditum est.''

It is impossible to have external authority for the conciliarity (''sobornost'') of the Church, for such an authority would thus become superior to the Church and to the spirit which lives in it. The Church is the Church, and that is the limit of the evidence for its identity with itself.

The conciliarity of the Church is much richer in content than everything which is manifest, ''explicit,'' in ecclesiastical doctrine. The actual dogma, the obligatory doctrine expounded in the symbolic books, always expresses a part of the Church's knowledge only. In the life of the Church there are certitudes which have never been defined dogmatically. There is, above all, the ''catholic'' consciousness of the Church, concerning which there has never been any dogma, although it would seem that such a dogma ought to be the foundation for all others. The Roman Church adopted its ''constitutio de ecclesia'' only in 1870, and even this does not contain a definition of the Church itself. All doctrines concerning the Mother of God and her cult (except the definition of the Third Ecumenical Council), the veneration of saints, the after life, the Last Judgment, the Church's ideas on the subject of life, of civilization, of creative activity and of many other things which the conciliarity of the Church contains and manifests, have never been dogmatically defined by Orthodoxy. The Church is its own self-evidence, the foundation of all definitions. It is the light which contains all the fullness of the spectrum, but which itself remains entirely white, inexpressible in other colors, like light in which all colors exist. The Church is indefinable, as is the Holy Spirit who lives in it. The Church is the Church, it includes all, but it is only within it, in its spirit, that ecclesiastical dogmas may be distinguished.

Sobornost is not only a passive preservation of the truth, it is also the active possession of that truth, the acceptance of the revelation of the spirit of God. In other words, conciliarity, as fact, implies "conciliation" as act, and this act takes place in time and manifests in part that which belongs to all. Conciliarity is a fact, not only of the mystical order, but of the historic order as well. It is the substratum of the history of the Church. It not only exists, but it is constantly active, thus continuing revelation in history and manifesting itself, through tradition or "dogmatic development." Sobornost is life and there is no place in life for immobility. The sobornost of the Church appears in its life and action earlier than in its consciousness. The Church is discovered actually to be in possession of a certain doctrine before it finds specific expression in a form of service, of prayer, or in an icon. Thus the veneration of the Virgin appeared before there was an official theological Mariology. It is not the dogma which prescribes Church practice, but the latter which is the foundation of the dogma.

Sobornost is the true, although hidden, source of the dogmatic knowledge of the Church, but its character is super-rational, intuitive—the means of "knowing" and "seeing." What, then, is its connection with dogma as truth expressed in rational terms? And what is dogma? The conscience of the Church is super-personal. Truth is revealed not to the individual mind, but to the unity in love of the Church. It is mysterious and unknown in its ways, like the descent of the Holy Spirit into human hearts. The integral nature of the Church's consciousness was manifest at Pentecost, at the moment of the foundation of the new Covenant. The Acts of the Apostles note very specially that the Spirit descended upon the

Apostles, all together and in unanimity. "They were all filled with the Holy Spirit" (Acts 2:1,4). The first preaching of St. Peter, which certainly might have been only personal, was also "catholic" by virtue of the "catholicity" of the Church. "And we all are witnesses" (Acts 2:32). In the same way, those who heard St. Peter, heard in him not a personal preacher, but all the Apostles: "In listening to these words they were touched to the heart and said to Peter and the rest of the Apostles, 'Brethren, what shall we do?' (Acts 2:37). It is said of the first community which was formed after Pentecost: "All who believed were together and had all things in common" (it is not necessary to understand "things" only as pertaining to goods in 5:45) "and day by day, attending the temple together (Acts 2:44, 46). This "together" is in general the norm of the spirit of the Church. It is a special quality of conciliarity, of integrality, which has no immediate quantitative value, but which means that individuality has been left behind for the attainment of a supreme spiritual, super-individual reality. The Church can exist "where two or three are gathered together" in the name of Christ. These ecclesiastical cells or local churches may, in fact, be ignorant one of another, with no direct relationship. But that is of no significance, for their unity in the spirit is in no way diminished. The same life in the Spirit is revealed in divers epochs and places. In a word, catholicity is the supreme reality of the Church, as the body of Christ. In the living experience of the unity of many in one, there appears what is known as conciliarity ("sobornost"), so that conciliarity is the only way and the only form of the Church. It is an unceasing miracle, the presence of the transcendent in the immanent, and, in that quality, can be an object of faith. The Church as truth is not given to individuals, but to a unity in love and faith it reveals itself as a supreme reality in which its members share in the measure of their "sobornost."

But, say the positivists (and there can be an ecclesiastical positivism), this is putting metaphysics above the Church: defining the Church as the limits of experience beyond the need for empirical gifts, regulated by the Canons. True, but the road leads from the metaphysical to the concrete and not the reverse. According to the meaning of the word "sobornost," the Church is not only an interior conciliarity, a life in the Holy Spirit, but also a collectivity which seeks the same spirit; the conciliar Church is also the Church of "conciliation." It is the Church of councils and especially the Church of local and ecumenical "conciliation" and unity of thought. The Church realizes its interior conciliarity by confession together and by ecclesiastical doctrine.

That which takes place in the super-consciousness beyond the limits of personal isolation, that which touches the supreme spiritual reality and inspires it, all this is repeated afterwards in the realm of reflection and personal consciousness; in other words, the super-conscious becomes conscious. Super-personal "catholic" experience becomes personal, crystallizes in thought, in knowledge, in fact, in contemplation and in speculation. The Greeks considered "wonder" as the principle of active philosophy. This wonder before the divine mysteries which are celebrated in the Church, is also the principle of active theology, both theoretical and practical. The songs of the Church tell of the wonder of the angels at the completion of divine destinies: "The angels, beholding the Dormition of the All-Pure Virgin, wondered." This wonder is the contemplation and the understanding of the divine mysteries. Religious truths have, first of all, a practical character; religion begins, not with theology, but with life in God; it is always connected with teaching, preaching and theology. The truth which reveals itself in life becomes the object of apperception by the mind and the will, in the measure of the personal and historic gifts of one or another individual. To the Galilean fishermen and to their humble followers was revealed the same truth as to St. Augustine, to St. Basil the Great, to St. Gregory of Nyssa, rich in Hellenic culture. The conscious assimilates what it receives from the super-conscious, from the conciliarity of the spirit of the Church. That spirit realizes its unity-in-many as a society, "societas." That is why the ecclesiastical consciousness is not an individual but a social work, "ecumenical" in the external sense of that word, or, more exactly, "conciliation."

The Church-society is also collectivity, tending naturally to collectivism in its own life. In this way the Church does not differ from other forms of social life, the state, the nation. Private associations tend toward a collective realization and expression of their will. The Church differs from them in that it believes a superhuman truth, given for its attainment, and it tends to union and to concord in the search for that truth. If the content is the same, the expression ought to be the same also—it is collectivism of thought which becomes a real mental uniformity revealed in the Church. Notwithstanding their resemblance, men never repeat each other; individual differences in the expression of the same content always exist. St. Paul has a remarkable expression in regard to these differences: "There must be factions among you in order that those who are genuine among you may be recognized" (I Cor. 11:19). "There must": by these words the Apostle not only testifies to the inevitability of many opinions, which already contained the possibility of separation (heresies), but he approves the final reason for that multiplicity. But variety of thought should not become difference of thought and should not lead to separation; the norm is unity of thought, which flows from love and from the "sobornost" of the Church, "one body in one spirit." It is natural and inevitable for the consciousness of the Church to realize a social communion in the works of faith. Common theological work corresponds with this, a work which consists in a continual exchange of opinions, and consequently of conciliation.

In sharing a unity of life, the Church tends necessarily to unity of thought and of doctrine. This unique doctrine within certain limits assumes a normative value and becomes the subject of preaching. The immediate and concrete experience of the Church contains the germ of dogma: from this experience dogma is born, as a definition of truth by means of words and ideas. This definition depends on historic circumstances. It is, in a certain sense, pragmatic. Dogma expresses a certain side of truth, sometimes for apologetic ends—to deny such or such an error, as for instance all the Christological dogmas. It is the answer of the Church to the question put by a certain epoch. And certainly such a pragmatic answer contains a general ecclesiastical truth, which could be found and given to humanity only by means of history. But, in spite of all their importance, it cannot be said that dogmas express the whole of the faith. They are only guide-posts on the road. A given experience contains in its depths much more than its oral, rational expression. ''Sobornaia'' consciousness cannot remain super-personal: it inevitably becomes personal experience, belonging to individuals. The character of feeling and consciousness varies with the individual, of course, whether he be man or child, layman or theologian. A personal, religious consciousness is given to each one, but once given, it may either remain confused or it may be enlarged and deepened. Hence arise theological thoughts and theological systems. Both are normal reflexes of an integral religious experience. A personal religious consciousness, personal theological thought, seeks to enlarge, to deepen, to affirm, to justify its faith and to identify it with the super-individual perception of the Church. This faith tends to be united with its primary source, the integral experience of the Church, attested by ecclesiastical tradition. This is why theological thought, which, in its quality of individual creative work and of individual perception in the Church, has necessarily an individual character, cannot and should not remain egotistically individual (for this is the source of heresy, of division), but should tend to become the theology of tradition and to find in the latter its justification. It is not that these thoughts should simply repeat in other words what already exists in tradition, as it seems to formal and narrow minds, the ''scribes and Pharisees'' of our day. On the contrary, that thought should be new, living and creative, for the life of the Church never stops and tradition is not a dead letter, but a living spirit. Tradition is living and creative: it is the new in the old and the old in the new. Each new theological thought, or more exactly each new expression, seeks justification, support in the tradition of the whole Church, in the largest sense of that word, including first of all Holy Scripture and after that oral and monumental tradition.

If the acts of the councils are studied it will be noted what space is occupied with the justification of each conciliar decision by testimony taken from tradition. This is why obedience to tradition and accord with it are the internal tests of individual consciousness in the Church.

Although different forms of "conciliation" can exist, outside of regular councils, nevertheless ecclesiastical assemblies or councils, in the real sense of the word, are the most natural and the most direct means of conciliation. This is just the place which the councils have always held in the life of the Church, beginning with the Council in Jerusalem. The councils are, above all, the tangible expression of the spirit of conciliarity and its realization. A council must not be considered as a wholly exterior institution, which, with the voice of authority, proclaims a divine or ecclesiastical law, a truth otherwise inaccessible to the isolated members of the Church. By a natural process the significance of the councils is determined in that they receive, later on, the authority of permanent ecclesiastical institutions. But the institution of canonical legislation, of "jus ecclesiasticum," has only a practical and not a dogmatic character. The Church, deprived, for one reason or another, of the possibility of convoking councils, does not cease to be the Church; and among other traits, it retains "sobornost," is conciliar, in the internal sense, for that is its nature.

Lacking councils, there yet remains the other means of "conciliation," for example, the direct relations between different local churches in apostolic times. It must be noted that, in our day, in the century of the development of the press and other means of circulation, councils have lost a great part of the utility of former times, such as those of the ecumenical councils. In our day ecumenical, universal conciliation is being realized almost imperceptibly, by means of the press and of scientific relations. But today the councils hold their special, unique place in conciliation because they alone offer the opportunity of immediate realization of the conciliarity of the Church. The meetings of representatives of the Church, in the cases where it is given to them to become ecclesiastical councils, actualize the conscience of the Church, in regard to some question which has been previously the object of personal judgment. These assemblies can demonstrate the conciliarity of the Church and become, consequently, true councils. Then, conscious of their true conciliarity and at the same time seeking it, the councils say of themselves: "It has pleased the Holy Spirit (who lives in the Church) and us." They consider themselves as identical with the Church where the Holy Spirit lives. Every ecclesiastical assembly expresses in its prayer the desire to become a council. But all ecclesiastical assemblies are not councils, however much they pretend to be or fulfill the exterior conditions requisite to that end, for example, the pseudo-councils of Ephesus, the iconoclastic council of 754, the council of Florence, which the Orthodox Church does not recognizes as councils. It must be remembered that even ecumenical councils are not external organs established for the infallible proclamation of the truth and instituted expressly for that. Such a proposition would lead to the conclusion that, without councils, the Church would cease to be "catholic" and infallible. Apart from this consideration, the mere idea of an external organ to proclaim the truth would place that organ above the Church, it would subordinate the action of the Holy Spirit to an external fact, such as an ecclesiastical assembly. Only the Church in its identity with itself can testify to the truth and the knowledge of conciliarity. Is a given assembly of bishops really a council of the Church which testifies in the name of the Church, to the truth of the Church? Only the Church can know. It is the Church which pronounces its silent yes (and sometimes not silent.) It is the Church which agrees, or not, with the council. There are not, and there cannot be, external forms established beforehand for the testimony of the Church about itself.

The life of the Church is a miracle which cannot be subordinated to external law. The Church recognizes or does not recognize a given ecclesiastical assembly representing itself as a council; this is the simple historical fact. Another historical fact is that to be accepted by the Church as such, it is not sufficient for an ecclesiastical assembly to proclaim itself as a council. It is not a question of a

juridical and formal acceptance. This does not mean that the decisions of the councils should be confirmed by a general plebiscite and
that without such a plebiscite they have no force. There is no such
plebiscite. But from historical experience it clearly appears that the
voice of a given council has truly been the voice of the Church or it
has not: that is all. There are not, there cannot be, external organs
or methods of testifying to the internal evidence of the Church; this
must be admitted frankly and resolutely. Anyone who is troubled
by this lack of external evidence for ecclesiastical truth does not
believe in the Church and does not truly know it. The action of the
Holy Spirit in the Church is an unfathomable mystery which fulfills
itself in human acts and human consciousness. The ecclesiastical
fetishism which seeks an oracle speaking in the name of the Holy
Spirit and which finds it in the person of a supreme hierarch, or in
the episcopal order and its assemblies—this fetichism is a terrible
symptom of half-faith.

The idea of ''sobornost'' implies a circle; the conciliarity of the
councils is proved by that of the Church, and the conciliar consciousness of the Church is proved by the Councils. But this logical
circle is not, practically, a vicious circle; it expresses only the identity of the Church with itself, in its manifestations. It may be asked,
where, when and how the ecumenicity of the councils is confirmed.
There is one easy answer: by the sanction of a supreme hierarchy.
This opinion finds no confirmation in history. It must be
remembered that the authority of conciliar decisions, even those of
ecumenical councils, from the very first was not considered as self-
evident, for these decisions were later confirmed. Almost every
ecumenical council confirmed, directly or indirectly, preceding
councils. This would be quite incomprehensible if the councils were
considered in themselves as exterior organs of infallibility.

We must then ask the following questions: to whom in the
Church belongs the power to proclaim doctrinal truth? To the
authority of the Church which is centered in the hands of the
episcopate. As a rule, the councils are composed of bishops. True,
this is not because of canon law which excludes the presence

of clergy and laity; on the contrary, the latter were present with the bishops at the Council of Moscow in 1917-18. The bishops take part in the councils as representatives of their dioceses—hence the rule that only diocesan bishops are present. They testify not "ex sese" but "ex consensu ecclesiae," and, in the persons of the bishops, it is the Church which participates in the councils.

But the doctrinal value of the council of bishops is not confined to rendering judgment; it is their province not only to offer opinions, but also to use their power to formulate necessary decisions and to proclaim dogmatic definitions, as is proved by the ecumenical and certain local councils. This sometimes gives the impression that the ecumenical council is the external organ of infallible judgment—a collective papacy with many heads. This opinion may be found in certain sections of Orthodox literature which have been subject to Catholic influence. It was the dominant theory at the time of the Catholic reform councils of Constance and Basle, where two external authorities, the Pope and the Councils, came into conflict. This theory contains much that is vague as to details; to what does the infallibility belong—to the episcopal dignity? But if each bishop is transformed into a pope there is always the possibility of a bishop becoming heretical. This is well proved by history. On the other hand, it is possible to have disagreements among bishops, and it is an historical fact that a doctrinal decision has never been rendered unanimously. It is true that the dissenting bishops at a given council were then anathematized and excommunicated, so that the unanimity of all the episcopate was insured. Nevertheless, it is well understood that such questions are not decided unanimously, but by the majority—what majority is unknown. Let us add the fact that only a certain portion of the episcopate was represented at the ecumenical councils and that the number of Eastern bishops was naturally predominant. Even the smallest number of bishops, however, may be the "conciliar" voice of the Church, if the Church recognizes them as such. But if an external authority is seen in the councils of the Church, the application of the principle of a collective papacy leads to greater difficulties than that of the papal monarchy.

Happily the idea of a collective papacy in the episcopate, taken as a whole, by no means expresses the Orthodox doctrine on the infallibility of the Church, for the episcopal dignity in itself does not confer dogmatic infallibility. A dogmatic judgment and its value depend more on sanctity than on dignity; the voice of a saint has more value than that of the regular clergy and bishops. The latter are doubly responsible for their judgments because they are invested with hieratic powers. Nevertheless a certain power to proclaim doctrinal definitions does belong to the council of bishops, this council being the supreme organ of ecclesiastical power. It is only in this aspect that ecumenical or local councils can legislate. The episcopal order possesses the authority to safeguard the purity of doctrine in the Church, and, in the case of profound differences in the heart of the Church, can render a decision having the force of laws. Such a decision should put an end to dissensions. Those who do not submit are automatically cut off from the Church by anathema. This has been the usual procedure in the history of the Church. The judgment of the councils of bishops is proclaimed by its presiding officer. For a national Church this is naturally its patriarch or its chief hierarch; for the ecumenical Church it is naturally the chief patriarch, ''primus inter pares''; the canons always recognized the bishops of Rome as such. The Orthodox world would still continue to accord that prerogative to the Pope, in his capacity of leading Ecumenical Patriarch, if he and his local Church would renounce their pretensions to primacy in the sense of the Vatican definitions. The Orthodox Church has never denied that primacy of the Roman See which was confirmed by the canons of the ecumenical councils.

We must distinguish between the proclamation of the truth, which belongs to the supreme ecclesiastical authority, and the possession of the truth which belongs to the entire body of the Church, in its catholicity and its infallibility. The latter is reality itself; the former is only a judgment passed on reality. This judgment—or dogma—has an abstract and pragmatic value, for it is the response of the Church to the questions of heretics or of those

who are in doubt. It possesses, so to speak, agreement with an absolute and supreme end, while not possessing concrete religious
plenitude which lives in the Church; it is a catalogue of the truth
and not the living truth itself. Neverthelss this dogmatic judgment
is indispensable as truth conceptually expressed and later as the
norm for the life of the Church. Here we must note the difference
between infallibility of the decisions of the Council of Chalcedon, for
example, and that of the multiplication table. We are dealing with
the same sort of distinction as between "the truth" and "the
fact." The infallibility of a given Church judgment consists in its
correspondence with the purpose of the Church, its accuracy in expressing truth in the given circumstance.

But, by its proclamation, the organ of ecclesiastical power does
not become of itself, "ex sese," the possessor of infallibility; that
belongs only to the Church in its ecumenicity. The ecclesiastical
authority (the council of bishops, or sometimes even a single bishop
in the limits of his diocese) is only the legal organ for the proclamation of the mind of the Church, the expression of the truth of the
Church, and becomes thus in a certain sense "pars pro toto." This
is why such judgment, though clothed in legal forms, must yet be
accepted by the Church as to its content. This may be accomplished
at the very moment of proclamation; then the dogmatic definition of
the council of bishops immediately attains an ecumenical character.
Nevertheless it may happen that even after the council its decisions
are not accepted; either for some time—as after the first council of
Nicea—or for ever, as in the case of the iconoclastic council of
Ephesus. These councils were then convicted of pseudo-
conciliarity. It develops that they were not true councils.

Thus a conflict may arise between certain members of the
Church and the ecclesiastical power. It follows that the dogmatic
definitions of the council are not received blindly, by virtue of the
duty of passive obedience. Rather it is by the activity of individual
conscience and intelligence, or by confidence in the council and
obedience to its proclamations, that these definitions are received as
expressing the truth of the Church. In such a way "conciliation"

takes place, not only before the council but also afterwards, for the reception or rejection of the conciliar decision. Such has always been the practice of the Church, and such is the dogmatic significance of the proclamation of dogmatic truth by the council. There is no place in the "sobornost" of the Church for a dogmatic oracle, either individual or collective. The Holy Spirit, Who lives in the Church, Himself points out the way to unanimity, and the decision of the council is only a method of achieving it. We thus face the following conclusion: As there exists on earth no external authority whatever—for Our Lord Jesus Christ, risen to heaven and become the invisible head of the Church, has left us none—the decisions of the councils have of themselves only a relative authority; that authority becomes absolute only by its reception in the universal Church. The Church has already vested with this infallibility the definitions of the seven ecumenical councils and of certain local councils, for example, the council of Carthage, and the councils of Constantinople of the fourteenth century, which established the doctrine of divine energies and of the "Light of Mt. Tabor."

This idea of an authority relatively infallible, represented by the legal organs of ecclesiastical power, beginning with the ecumenical council and ending with the diocesan bishop in the limits of his diocese—this idea, to Catholics and those who would ecumenize the Church, may appear contradictory and even destructive. A certain contradiction may seem to be inherent here, for the submission of definitions to the consent of the faithful and the adhesion of the faithful to the definitions are simultaneously recognized as obligatory. On the one hand the orders of the ecclesiastical canon represented by the episcopate should be obeyed ("ecclesiam in episcopo esse," St. Cypr, ep. 66). Dogmatic definitions must be included among such orders. But the obligation does not derive from the infallible authority of the episcopate united in council "ex sese"; it derives from the right of the episcopal power to conserve doctrine, to guard its integrity and to proclaim the definitions obligatory for the Church.

This obedience should not be blind, it should not be the result of fear. It should be an act of conscience, and it is obligatory in so far as it is not directly opposed to the dictates of conscience. When the Apostles Peter and Paul were led to the Sanhedrin, which for them was still the legal and supreme ecclesiastical power, and were arraigned before the elders and the chief priests, and when these latter commanded them to cease preaching the Christ, they answered: "Whether it is right in the sight of God to listen to you rather than to God, you must judge" (Acts 4:19). This example should guide us. The dogmatic definition of a council, vested with the fullness of ecclesiastical power, certainly has a supreme authority for believers, and should be obeyed, even in doubtful and obscure cases. But there may be instances where, precisely, disobedience to ecclesiastical power or to a council, which had become heretical, is glorified by the Church. This happened, for example, in the times of the Arian, Nestorian and Iconoclastic discords. Such cases are, of course, exceptions; but were there only one, it would have great dogmatic value in principle, because it nullifies the case for an external infallibility above the Church such as Catholics ascribe to the Pope.

It may be asked, perhaps, where and when this doctrine of the conciliarity of the Church was developed, it must be answered that this idea has never been officially expressed in words, just as it is equally impossible to find in patristic literature any special doctrine concerning the Church. Nevertheless, the contrary doctrine, that of an external organ of infallibility, has no more been expounded unless one takes into account certain isolated expressions, evidently inexact and exaggerated, in Irenaeus, Cyprian, Ignatius of Antioch. But the practice of the Church, that is, all the history of the councils, presupposes the idea of conciliarity, of "sobornost." The opposition to Roman pretensions, which later arose, made this still more evident.

Thus it may be said that the supreme ecclesiastical power, under the form of a council of bishops—ecumenical, national, or even diocesan—has, in practice, the right to declare necessary doctrinal definitions and that these definitions ought to be accepted, barring exceptional and specially justified cases. Disobedience to ecclesiastical power is in itself a grave fault, a heavy burden on the conscience, even though it is sometimes inevitable. Thus the higher leadership of the Church is vested with an authority, ''infallible'' in practice, which is sufficent for the needs of the Church. It is not so much a legal power as an authority born of love. Church history rightly testifies that such is the character of the supreme leadership of the Church. Otherwise it would be impossible to comprehend the history of the councils and their dogmatic definitions, which did not always or immediately put an end to dissensions, but which led little by little to unanimity. In practice such a ''system without system'' is altogether sufficient; it possesses the advantage of uniting liberty with obedience to the Church.

The absence of an external infallible authority in matters of doctrine, and the possibility of relatively infallible definitions by ecclesiastical authority, definitions which express the catholic conscience of the Church, this is the palladium of Orthodox liberty. It is at the same time the cause of the greatest astonishment: to Catholics a stumbling-block and folly to Protestants. The latter place above all the personal search for the truth, a principle whose value cannot be overestimated in Christianity; they cannot understand the necessity of placing their own subjectivity beneath the objectivity of the Church, of testing the former by the latter. For them the doctrine of the Church identifies itself completely with their personal opinions, or at least with the consensus of such opinions. Ecclesiastical tradition, contained by the whole Church in common, simply does not exist for them. But proceeding from these ideas, it is possible to approach the idea of conciliarity, or, at least, there are no obstacles. The agreement of personal subjective opinions may be understood as the objective ecumenical truth, as its manifestation. Hence it is possible for Protestantism, full of the spirit of liberty, to understand Orthodox conciliarity, ''sobornost.'' As a matter of fact, Protestantism itself contains the idea of an authority relatively infallible in matters of doctrine. The assembly of synods which fixed the profession of faith, such as the Augsburg confession, are nothing but ecclesiastical organs endowed with relatively infallible

authority and accepted by the Church. And the sources of ecclesiastical conciliation which are appearing in our day (the conference of Lausanne included), are they not the beginning of a way,
not yet clearly perceived from the dogmatic point of view, but
already accepted and sanctioned by life?

The idea of sobornost encounters much more opposition on the
part of Catholics. This is quite comprehensible, after the proclamation of the Vatican dogma. For them, it is the synonym of anarchy
in the Church and even of spiritual slavery, because "personal
liberty, not controlled by authority, would be slavery." Obedience
"for itself," or blind obedience, is entirely in its place and natural
in a monastery, for "the suppression of the will" is the very condition of monasticism, so to speak, its spiritual method. But the essential thing here is that the path of obedience has been freely chosen
by the monk. In this sense the most absolute monastic obedience,
accepted with the monastic vows, is really an act of supreme Christian liberty—although even here obedience does not free one from a
Christian conscience and its responsibilities, should not become
blind: if the "starets" (superior) or spiritual director becomes
heretical, the bonds of obedience are broken at once. But in the
Roman Church obedience to the Pope is obligatory for all, and in all
the life of the Church—in all that concerns faith, morals, canonical
discipline. An obedience without reserve is demanded, not only exterior, but interior. The necessity for blind obedience by all, to an
external authority, is a system of spiritual slavery, incompatible
with Christian liberty. Subjectively this slavery may sometimes be
softened by filial devotion to the Holy Father, and we do not doubt
that such is often the case. Spiritual filiality toward hierarchs has
analogous manifestations in Orthodoxy as well as in Catholicism.
But relationships within the Church are not limited to this sentiment. Its predominance condemns the Church to a sort of infan-
tilism or spiritual minority; all responsibility and all initiative in the
Church devolves upon its head. This is impossible in the life of the
Church. It is impossible even in Catholicism, which saves itself by
its inconsistencies from the dead hand of the Vatican dogma.

It may be said that to enter or not to enter the Church is in itself an act of liberty which by that very fact makes obedience to the Pope a consequence. But this would be only a subterfuge. "Extra ecclesiam nulla salus"; and it is only in the Church that a Christian life is possible. If life in the Church implies obedience to an authority conceived as the living incarnation of the Church, the Pope, this is to say that the Christian life excludes liberty and is founded on blind obedience to an external authority. The existence of an external infallible authority in the Church is incompatible with personal liberty and makes of obedience to authority an act, not of blind submission, but of personal conviction, by which there is discovered the truth in the conscience of the whole Church.

But it must not be thought that, because of this principle, Orthodoxy becomes an arena where personal opinions are opposed to each other, opinions endowed with as subjective a value as those of Protestantism. Is not such liberty anarchy, a personal arbitrariness? Doubtless such a tendency is always possible, but as personal abuse, as sin against the Church.

Yet, for a member of the Orthodox Church, there exists a truth of the Church. Each one should seek to perceive this by his own effort. And each ought to strive towards agreement with the Church in his subjective experience, without which striving there can be no partaking of the truth of the Church, and in the objectivity of Church tradition. The former preserves one from a desiccated rationalism, and without it an approach to truth is impossible. The latter impels the believer to bring his individual conscience into the objective ecclesiastical tradition, into the stream of the whole Church. The interior norm of the search for the truth is the justification of one's personal opinion by the tradition of the Church.

Finally, there is the judgment of ecclesiastical authority. It has the power to enforce measures of canonical discipline; it is called upon to act against those who do not think according to the norm. The history of the Church testifies sufficiently to this. This is why the idea that in Orthodoxy there exists no theological norm valid for the whole Church, but that each one is guided only by his own opinions, is altogether false. It is true, however, that in comparison with the Roman confession, Orthodoxy leaves more liberty to personal theological thought, to individual judgment in the domain of "theological opinions" ("theologoumena"). This is a consequence of the fact that Orthodoxy, while safeguarding essential dogmas, necessary to the faith, knows no theological doctrine obligatory for all. It applies the principle: "in necessariis unitas, in dubiis libertas."

In general the tendency of Orthodox doctrine is not to increase the number of dogmas beyond the limits of the purely indispensable. In the realm of dogma, Orthodoxy rather makes her own rule, "not to govern or dogmatize too much." The plenitude of life contained in the life of the Church is not completely expressed by the obligatory dogmas it professes; these are rather bounds or indications beyond which Orthodox doctrine ought not to go, negative definitions more than positive. It is false to think that established dogma, "dogma explicita," exhausts all doctrine, i.e. "dogma implicita." On the contrary, the domain of doctrine is much more vast than that of existing definition. It can even be said that definitions can never exhaust doctrine, because dogmas have a discursive, rational character, while the truth of the Church forms an indissoluble whole. This does not mean that the truth cannot be expressed by concepts; on the contrary, the fullness of truth opens to us an inexhaustible theological source. These theological thoughts, which, in the case of mystics and ascetics, have an intuitive character, receive an expression more rational and more philosophical from theologians. It is the legitimate domain of individual creative work, which should not be bound by doctrine.

Sometimes subjective narrowness can lead to error. This is then corrected by the consciousness of the Church, as expressed in "sobornost," but there cannot and there should not be a unique theological doctrine, obligatory for all, as taught by Thomism. For theology and its teachings are not identical with the dogmatic. Forgetting that difference gives rise to much misunderstanding. The measures taken by Rome against "modernism" tend to hold

all theology in the narrow confines of official doctrine, and that inevitably produced hypocrisy. Liberty in these spheres is the very life
of theological thought. The ancient Church knew various schools of
theology, and many very different theological individualities. It may
be said that in the spiritual life this variety is most useful when it is
greatest. Even in Catholicism, thanks to the luxuriant growth of
theological science, there exist diverse currents of theological
thought belonging to different monastic orders. Orthodox theology
in Russia, in the nineteenth century and in our day, contains a
whole series of original theological individualities, which resemble
each other very little and which are all equally Orthodox. The
Metropolitan Philaret and A.J. Bukharev, Khomiakov and V.
Soloviev, Dostoevsky and Konstantin Leontiev, Fr. Florensky and
N.A. Berdyaev and others, despite many differences, express, each
in his own way, the Orthodox conscience, in a sort of theological
rhapsody. Here lies the beauty and the strength of Orthodoxy, and
not its weakness, as Catholic theologians and even sometimes Orthodox hierarchs ready to transform their personal opinions into
theological norms, are inclined to think. For Orthodoxy such
pretensions are only abuse, or a falling into error. Orthodox
theology developed marvellously in the East and in the West, before
the separation of the Churches. After the separation it continued to
develop in Byzantium, up to the end of the Empire, and it has continued that tradition down to the present day in Greek theology. Orthodox thought has been undergoing an entirely original renaissance in the Russian theology of the nineteenth and twentieth
centuries, and, although at present suppressed in Russia by force, it
continues to flourish in the emigration.

It should be said of Orthodox theological thought that it is far
from having been exhausted in the classic times of the patristic
period or later on in Byzantium: a glorious future opens before it.
Orthodoxy is only now beginning to express itself in contemporary
language and for the contemporary conscience. All this by no
means lessens the unique value of the patristic period. But sincere
theology must be modern, that is, it must correspond with its

epoch. Our epoch has seen colossal revolutions in all the domains of thought, of knowledge, and of action. These revolutions wait a response on the part of Orthodox theology. Our time cannot be satisfied with an archaic or medieval scholastic theology. This new development will continue in the lines of Orthodox tradition. But fidelity to tradition is not an artificial and insincere stylization. True fidelity is a right perception of the old in the new, a sense of their organic connection. The patristic works can be considered only as monuments of the Orthodox conscience of a given historical period. These works are the testimony to the Church given by the holy fathers in the language of their time, which differs perceptibly from ours. It follows that an unlimited development of Orthodox dogmatics is possible—not a development of dogmas themselves, for they are not open to that, but of their interpretation and expression. Will this richness of thought be limited to the conciliar definitions, obligatory for all, and will these definitions be limited to those of the seven ecumenical councils? It is impossible to say, and the answer to this question is of no decisive importance. What is important is that conciliarity, the catholic conscience of the Church, should be in movement and that it should be enriched as we advance in human history. And the new contact of the peoples of the West with the Orthodox conscience, as well as the contact of Eastern theology with the theological thought of the West, promises a lofty and rich future for Orthodox theology. This future exists in the depths of the consciousness of the Church and towards it we are moving.

All these properties of Orthodoxy, connected with its "sobornost," its conciliarity, result in its indefinable character, its unfinished state, if we may use the term. This is the impression received when Orthodox thought is compared with Latin precision. Very often, in questions of a secondary order, where Orthodoxy offers only theological opinions or devotional habitude, the Roman Church presents either dogmas completely formulated, or at least doctrines officially fixed, for instance, in the teaching about the future life, in its various phases. Some may think that this is an ad-

vantage and that the absence of such precision is a sign of weakness
and immaturity. We do not deny this fact of incompleteness, which
finds its partial explanation in the historic destinies of Orthodoxy.
But fundamentally these traits are inherent in the Church as a
whole, because its life has depths which are quite unfathomed. The
finished character of a religious system does not always proceed
from an interior maturity, but sometimes from the fact that
everything in it has taken the form of pragmatic dogmas, violently
and prematurely. This is easy for the feeble, but it fetters the
Christian spirit, for this spirit is ever striving onward and upward.
For "where the Spirit of the Lord is, there is freedom" (2 Cor.
3:17).

CHAPTER 4

THE UNITY OF THE CHURCH

The Church is one. This is an ecclesiological axiom, evident for every Christian: "There is one body and one spirit, as you have been called to the one hope that belongs to your call. There is one Lord, one faith, one baptism, one God and Father of us all" (Eph. 4:4-6). When the Church is spoken of in the plural, therefore, it is for the purpose of recording the existence of many local Churches within the one Church, or of pointing out that there are different confessions, which have a separate existence in the heart of the same Apostolic Church. Such an expression is certainly inadequate and must not lead to error. Just as there cannot exist several Truths (although the Truth may have many aspects), so there cannot be many "Churches." There is only one true Church, the Orthodox Church. The question of the interior unity of a plurality of "churches" and of their relation to the Church will be studied later. It must be stated at the outset that in spite of plurality of historical forms in the one Church, an essential pluralism is inadmissible. According to the theory of "branches of the Church" the one Church is operating differently, but in equal measure, in the different "branches" of historic Christianity: Orthodoxy, Catholicism, Anglicanism. This theory leads to the conclusion that the tradition of the true Church exists everywhere and nowhere. This brings us to the idea of a "church invisible," the concept of the Church lost in historic relativity. Because of the multiplicity of gifts and of the achievements of historic Christianity the unchangeable unity and the continuity of tradition preserved by the Orthodox Church is often unnoticed.

This being granted, another question arises: how is it that each ecclesiastical society considers itself to be the true Church? Human narrowness, ignorance and error are surely the cause; but on the other hand the fact also bears witness to the real contact of each of these ecclesiastical societies with the Church, in its deepest sense. It is only in the center, that the situation of all points of the circumference may be observed, and it is only in being part of the true Church, unique and spotless, that one can understand the truth, the falsity, or the limited character of the Churches which claim, each one, to be the whole of the one Church. Orthodoxy is that one true Church which preserves the continuity of the life of the Church, that is, the unity of tradition. To admit that this one true Church no longer exists on earth, but that its branches contain the parts, is to abandon belief in the promise of Our Lord, Who said the forces of hell should not prevail against the Church. This would be acknowledging that to preserve the purity and thus the unity of the Church had been something beyond human power, that the foundation of the Church upon the earth had not succeeded. This is a lack of faith in the Church and its Head. Consequently it must be understood, first of all, that the unity of the Church means the true Church without spot, that it is unique on earth. But this does not deny to the churches (in the plural) a certain degree of the true spirit of the Church. In speaking of the unity of the Church, the absolute character of that idea must be confirmed, and the relativity of the different historic forms of the Church (the churches) can be explained only in the light of that affirmation. The Church is one and consequently unique, and this one unique Church, this true Church, which possesses the truth without spot, and in its plenitude (although that plenitude may not be entirely manifest in history) is Orthodoxy. The doctrine of the unity of the Church is connected with the unity of Orthodoxy, and with the special form of that unity.

The unity of the Church is both internal and external. The internal unity of the Church corresponds to the unity of the body of Christ and of the life of the Church. Life in the Church is above all a mysterious life in Christ, and with Christ, a unity of life with all creation, communion with all human beings, of whom the saints are the chief on earth and in heaven, and also with the world of angels (vide Heb. 12:22-23). It is life in the Church, and consequently must be defined, first of all, qualitatively and not quantitatively.

This quality, the unity of the life of the Church as the body of Christ, is manifested by a certain identity of life (unity of ecclesiastical experience) among its members, a oneness not dependent on this external unity and even, in a certain sense, preceding it. Those unknown to the world and who know it not—hermits and anchorites—live in the unity of the Church just as much as those who live in organized ecclesiastical societies. This internal unity is the foundation of the external unity.

According to the Orthodox belief, this idea is expressed in the words of the Lord, addressed to Peter after the latter's confession of faith, a confession which he uttered as coming from all the Apostles. "You are Peter and on this rock I will build my Church" (Matt. 16:18), said the Master. Orthodoxy understands the rock of Peter to be the faith he confessed and shared with all the Apostles, an inner unity of the true faith and life. In Catholicism these words are understood as the institution of an external unity through the unique authority of Peter in the Church. But this unity in the life of the Church as a special interior quality reveals itself exteriorly, in the life of the historical, militant Church on earth. Unity is manifested by unity of faith and conscience, by doctrine, by the unity of prayer and sacraments; and thus by unity of tradition and by a unique ecclesiastical organization founded on the latter. The unity of the Church can manifest itself in two ways, in unity of life and faith, and in unity of organization, and these two sorts of unity must be in harmonious agreement. Now the idea of internal unity may gain predominance, now that of external unity. Accordingly, there are two types of Church unity, the Eastern Orthodox type and the Roman Catholic. According to the first, the Church is one by virtue of its unity of life and doctrine, even making an abstraction of external unity or of organization, which may or may not exist. For the Roman Church, where a sort of assimilation of Roman law and Christianity is realized, the ecclesiastical organization possesses decisive value. The Church exists in the unity of ecclesiastical power in the hands of its unique representative; in a word, unity is realized by the Pope of Rome, and by the loyalty of the whole Church of the whole universe to him.

Orthodox unity, on the contrary, is realized in the world in a diffuse manner, not by unity of power over the entire universal Church, but by unity of faith, and, growing out of this, unity of life and of tradition, hence also the apostolic succession of the hierarchy. This internal unity exists in the solidarity of the entire Christian world, in its different communities, independent but by no means isolated from one another. These communities recognize reciprocally the active force of their life of grace and of their hierarchy; they are in communion by means of the sacraments (intercommunion). Such a form of Church unity existed in Apostolic times; the Churches, founded by the Apostles in different cities and different countries, maintained a spiritual communion. This they expressed especially by their salutations, as in the Epistles of St. Paul: "All the Churches of Christ greet you" (Rom. 16:16), by mutual aid, above all to the Church in Jerusalem, and, in case of need, by direct relations and by councils.

This type of unity of the Church, a unity in plurality, was established because it alone corresponded to the Church's true nature. It is the system of national autocephalous Churches, living in union and mutual accord. Their union is above all doctrinal and sacramental. The autocephalous Churches confess the same faith and are sustained by the same sacraments: they are, when outward conditions permit, in sacramental communion. Then they have canonical relations. This means that each of the autocephalous Churches recognizes the canonical validity of the hierarchy of all the other Churches. While the hierarchy of each autocephalous Church is entirely independent in the exercise of its ministry, it is joined by this mutual recognition with, and finds itself under the silent observation of, the hierarchy of the entire Orthodox world. This does not often appear when ecclesiastical life is normal, but becomes evident in the case of any violation. Then the hierarchy of an autocephalous Church lifts its voice to defend Orthodoxy which has been transgressed by another Church. Different Churches intervene. In one way or another, by correspondence, the interrupted union becomes reestablished, or else a schism is formed which sometimes becomes permanent. The history of the Church bears witness to this in the discussions concerning Easter, discussion on the "lapsed," the Arian, Nestorian, Eutychian, and pneumatological disputes. This, by the way, is not all in agreement with the Catholic point of view, according to which an intervention of this sort, such a right of defence of ecumenical Orthodoxy, belongs to the Roman See only (the latter, strangely enough, remained aloof from the most important Arian discussions).

The smallest of the institutional unities of which the ecumenical Church is composed is the diocese. This clearly follows from the place in the Church belonging to the bishop: "nulla ecclesia sine episcopo." In exceptional circumstances, such as a time of persecution, a local Church may be deprived of its bishop or separated from him for some time, yet does not cease to form part of the body of the Church. But such an exception, which cannot last long, only confirms the general rule. History and canon law indicate that the local Churches, in each of which a bishop is the center, form part of a new canonical unity more complex, at the head of which is found the council of bishops and the primate. As ecclesiastical organization developed, there have been formed, "jure ecclesiastico," archbishoprics, metropolitanates, patriarchates, possessing, in the person of a leading hierarch, a chief priest invested with special powers, specially defined but by no means unlimited. In this way there arose in the ancient Church the pentarchy of patriarchal Churches which the canons of the Church have always ranged in order of dignity: Rome, Constantinople, Alexandria, Antioch and Jerusalem. These canons are formally in force in our day, but have actually become archaic, partly because of the Roman schism, partly because historical changes have greatly diminished the importance of the Eastern patriarchates. This last fact is allied with the formation of new patriarchates, among which first place certainly belongs to that of Russia. More recently other patriarchates have been created in Serbia, in Rumania, in Georgia, as well as many new autocephalous Churches after the Great War.

Thus ecclesiastical history shows that the independence of different Churches is no obstacle to their canonical union. This union is evidenced, in certain extraordinary instances, by councils composed of representatives of different Churches testifying certainly to their interior union—or by special hieratic agencies which express that unity. Such agencies are the patriarchs in general and above all the first of the patriarchates—that of Rome, especially before the separation. After the separation, the primacy devolved upon the second patriarchate, that of Constantinople, but this primacy is more a primacy ''de facto'' than a canonical primacy, not to mention the fact that the ''specific gravity'' and historical importance of the see of Constantinople were entirely changed after the fall of Byzantium. In the universal Church primacy of jurisdiction never belonged to any patriarch, even to the Roman; there was only a primacy of honor (''primus inter pares'') or of authority. In fact, doubtless, authority is sometimes power, but a spiritual, not a canonical power. Primacy in the council belonged to the Pope, although in fact the Pope was always represented in the ecumenical councils only by his legates. It was equally the province of the Pope to proclaim the definitions of the councils, to preside at the ecumenical synod if one were formed, and to be the symbolic representative of the unity of the Church. This unity naturally tended to become personified. Since the Roman schism, the ecumenical Church has had no individual head, and up to the present time, has felt no special need of one. If such a need were felt, it would be easily satisfied by applying old canons or by legislating new, a procedure entirely possible since the central ecclesiastical organization is formed not at all ''jure divino'' (as Catholics affirm concerning the papal primacy), but ''jure ecclesiastico,'' and more definitely ''modo historico.'' This organization may be changed according to the needs of the time. The canonical vestment of the Church is woven on the loom of history, although always in accordance with the Church's divine foundations.

The autocephalous organization of the Orthodox Churches leaves intact the concrete historic diversity which corresponds to the many nationalities within it. Our Lord said: "Go and teach all people." This gives to nationality its right of existence, its historic originality, joined nevertheless to the unity of life in the Church. The first preaching of the Apostles, one in its content, sounded forth in all languages, and each people heard it in its own tongue. In the same way the autocephalous national Churches preserve their concrete historical character; they are able to find their own forms of expression. It must be granted that this variety involves certain troublesome consequences, some very marked differences, but these things do not destroy unity; rather, they transform it from within. The multiple concrete unity of which, in the Book of Revelations, the Churches of Asia are the type, still remain the ideal of the Church. Its opposite is the Roman idea of an abstract unity, supernational or extra-national, which, in its practical realization, tends to incarnate itself in a special pontifical state. This state does not confine itself to the Vatican City, but would, if that were possible, expand to include the entire world. From the Roman point of view, the unity of the Church is the unity of administration concentrated in the hands of the Pope, a spiritual monarchy of the centralist type. The numerous practical advantages of such a clear absolutism are incontestable: at the price of obligatory uniformity more equality is attained, and the general level of life in the Church is higher. But these advantages are bought too dearly, at the price of transforming the Church of Christ into an earthly domain. The plurality of autocephalous Churches brings into the life of the Church more inequality and difference of opinion; it leads to an inevitable provincialism which, however, is fast disappearing in the face of the levelling process of culture in the civilized world of our day. We have here the natural limit imposed by history. In any case, second-rate goods cannot be bought, like Esau's mess of pottage, at the price of birth-right. A worldly autocracy cannot be substituted for Christian unity.

A natural rapprochment of peoples and of national Churches can remedy all existing inconveniences. Now that the life of historic humanity tends irresistibly toward unification, the Church is more and more vividly aware of the principles of universal ecumenicity; the idea of centralized authority, even as a force making for unity, is losing ground. Though the value of this process is not identical with the general democratization of life, it is parallel with it. Liberty becomes as indispensable as air; contemporary humanity cannot breathe without it. And the decentralized organization of Orthodoxy, that co-existence of national churches, autonomous but united, corresponds much more with the contemporary spirit than the centralization of Rome, whose desire to join all Churches under its rule becomes daily more and more Utopian. To save the Christian world from the infinite subdivision to which Protestantism leads and from despotic uniformity as advocated by Rome—this is the vocation of Orthodoxy. The Orthodox concept of unity has preserved for local Churches their own originality, their particular aspect, and at the same time it has maintained the unity of tradition. Such is unity in the Church, as Orthodoxy understands it. It is unity in multiplicity, a symphony in which many motives and voices are harmonized.

CHAPTER 5

THE SANCTITY OF THE CHURCH

The Church is holy. This quality of the Church is self-evident. Should not the body of Christ be holy? The sanctity of the Church is that of Christ Himself. The word of the Old Testament: "Be holy, for I am holy" (Lev. 11:44) is realized in the New Testament by means of the Incarnation, which is the santification of the human race by the Church. The sanctification of the Church, accomplished by the blood of Christ, has been realized by the Holy Spirit, which was poured into it at Pentecost, and lives for ever in the Church. The Church is the house of God, as our bodies are the temples of the holy Spirit. Thus life in the Church is sanctity in both an active and a passive sense: in the fact of sanctification and our acceptance of it. Life in the Church is a supreme reality in which we participate and by means of which we become sanctified. Sanctity is the very being of the "spirit of the Church." It may even be said that the latter has no other characteristics. Life in God, deification, sanctity, are the evident marks of the spirit of the Church, its synonyms. The apostolic writings call Christians "saints": "all the saints"—such is the name habitually given to members of Christian communities (2 Cor. 1:1; Eph.1:1; Phil. 1:1, etc.).

Does this mean that those communities were particularly holy? It is sufficient to remember Corinth. No, this term applies to the quality of life in the Church; everyone sharing in that life confesses sanctity. And this is true not only for the time of the Apostles, but for all the existence of the Church, for Christ is one and unchangeable, as is the Holy Spirit.

This question of the sanctity of the Church was asked, and the Church gave the answer, at the time of the struggle against Montanism and Donatism. The relaxation of the discipline of penance caused such a reaction amongst the Montanists that they, in overweening pride, began to preach a new doctrine according to which

95

the Church should be a society of perfect saints. In the same way the Church rejected the idea of the Donatists, which made the efficacy of the sacraments depend upon the moral value of its administrants, thus undermining faith in the sacraments themselves. Warring against Montanism and Novatianism, the Church defined the principle that its membership includes not only the good grain but also the tares. In other words it is composed of sinners to be saved: "If we say that we have no sin, we deceive ourselves and the truth is not in us" (1 John 1:8). In opposition to Donatism, the Church decided that sanctification is conferred in the sacrament by all ministers validly constituted, not by virtue of their personal sanctity, but by action of the Holy Spirit, living in the Church.

The Church is objectively holy by the power of the life divine, the sanctity of God, of the angels and of the saints in glory; but it is holy also by the sanctity of its members who are now living and who are now being saved. Sanctity in its primary, objective meaning is given to the Church, it is its divine side. And this sanctity cannot be taken away nor diminished by any human effort. This is grace, in the precise meaning of the word. Above all, the Church is called holy with reference to the power of sanctification it possesses. The action of this power extends to the life of humanity fallen in sin; the Light shines in the darkness. Salvation is, fundamentally, a process, in which light is separated from darkness and sin is vanquished. In attaining a certain quantitative degree, victory over sin accomplishes a qualitative change as well, as a result of which the sinner becomes just and holy.

There are always many saints in the Church, but they are not always known to the world; in the Church, "the golden circle" of saints is never broken. To admit the contrary would be to think that the Church has begun to lose its gifts of grace. But the sanctity of man, however great, is never complete sinlessness. Perfect holiness belongs only to God; in the light of that holiness, "his angels he charges with error" (Job 4:18). Hence the criterion of absolute sanctity is not applicable to man, and concerning man, only relative holiness may be spoken of. This ideal of human, relative sanctity should be obligatory on all the members of the Church. But then it must be asked, what is the degree of sanctity below which members of the Church cannot descend? This consideration is the basis of a certain discipline in the Church whose exigencies are binding upon all. Different epochs show a corresponding difference in the rigor of definition of these exigencies. The sects (ancient and modern Montanists) wished to limit the number of members of the Church by establishing the most severe rules (absence of "mortal sin"). The Church, on the other hand, applied a more indulgent discipline. The question of greater or less severity in discipline has, in itself, great importance. Whatever the solution, it is always essential that personal sinfulness should not forcibly separate a member from the Church and from its sanctity. In the works of Hermas, for example, we find that characteristic expression: "To the saints who have sinned" (Pastor vis. 11:24). What is of decisive importance is not complete freedom from sin, but the road that leads toward it. The man whose sin separates him from the Church remains in union with the Church so long as he follows the way of salvation and receives the sanctifying grace. Thus the sinner, also, who lives in the life of the Church, is holy; it may even be said that the Church knows no other saints than these.

Of course, there are limits to sanctity, high and low: sometimes saints are recognized and honored in their lifetime (although definite canonization is possible only after death); in other cases, certain members of the Church are cut off by the sword of excommunication, especially in cases of dogmatic deviations. But the great mass of those who are being saved and who are neither white nor black, but grey, remain in the Church and share its sanctity. And faith in the reality of that sanctifying life justly allows the Church to call all its members holy: "Holy things to holy people," proclaims the priest, while breaking the bread for the communion of the faithful. To oppose themselves, in the role of saints, to the Christian world fallen in sin, as the members of some sects claim to do, is phariseeism. No one knows the mysteries of the judgment of God, and it will be said to certain who prophesied and worked miracles in

the name of the Lord: "I never knew you" (Matt. 7:22-3). When
we speak of the sanctity of the Church, it is first of all the sanctity
conferred by the Church; the sanctity attained or realized by its
members comes only after that. It is indubitable that sanctity, true
divine holiness, does not exist outside the Church, and is conferred
by it alone.

From this it may be inferred that sanctity is generally invisible
and unknown and that, in consequence, the true Church is also invisible and unknown. But such a conclusion, accepted by Protestantism, would be false, because then the Church would be considered
only as a society of saints, and not as a power objectively given, a
power of sanctity and of divine life as the body of Christ. This life is
given, although invisibly, still in visible forms, and in view of this
given sanctifying power, the Church cannot be considered invisible.
It is given to the conscience of the Church, not to personal but to
collective conscience, to know the saints within it who have been
pleasing unto God and who have won, in themselves, the victory
over sin. The Church has knowledge of them in their life. After
their death this knowledge becomes certain, and that is canonization. Doubtless, many things still remain unknown to humanity,
and in this sense it is possible to speak of the unknown Church. The
idea is expressed by the Church itself when it celebrates the feast of
All Saints, that is, saints known or unknown. But this limitation of
knowledge is not the same thing as invisibility of the Church. From
the holiness of the Church it follows that there are instances where
certain of its members are glorified for their sanctity. A vivid example of this occurs when the Church canonizes a saint. There comes
a time when the Church changes the character of the prayer which
relates to a certain person. Instead of praying for the repose of his
soul and for the pardon of his sins, instead of praying for him, the
Church begins to address itself to him, asking his intercession for us
before God by his prayers. He has no further need of our prayers.
At the moment of the glorification of the saints, during the solemni-
ty of their canonization, there is a decisive and solemn time when
instead of the prayer for the glorified saint: "Give rest, O Lord, to

the soul of thy servant, ''there is heard, for the first time, a prayer addressed to the new saint: ''Holy Father, pray to God for us.''

According to the belief of the Church, the relations of love with the saints already glorified by God are not interrupted by death. On the contrary the saints, in constant relation with us, pray for us and aid us in all of our life. Certainly their life—a life of glory and of divine love—knows neither division nor isolation. They are in mysterious relations of love with the glorified Church and with the earthly militant Church. This is the communication of saints. It is not a communication of works ''of superogation,'' which idea is not recognized by the Orthodox Church; it is loving aid and assistance, an intercession by prayer, a participation takes place and remains veiled in the doctrine of the Church, as one of the mysteries of the beyond. The Church believes that angels guard the world and human life and are the instruments of Providence, that the saints take part in the life of man on earth, but this participation is hidden from mortal eyes. In particular, the Russian Church, in these days of terrible persecution, believes that Saint Sergius and Saint Seraphim, together with other saints of God, never cease to pray to Him in the interest of their suffering brethren.

CHAPTER 6

ORTHODOX DOGMA

The Orthodox Church has only a small number of dogmatic definitions, forming the profession of faith obligatory for all its members. Strictly speaking, this minimum consists of the Nicene-Constantinopolitan Creed, which is read during the baptismal service and the liturgy, and the definitions of the seven ecumenical councils. This does not mean that these documents exhaust all the doctrine of the Church; but the rest has not been so formulated as to become obligatory dogma for all. This remainder consists in theological teaching, treating particularly important questions, such as the cult of the Holy Virgin and the saints, the sacraments, salvation, eschatology, etc. This is, in general, the Orthodox method of approach; it contents itself with the indispensable minimum of obligatory dogmas. It is the opposite of Roman Catholicism which tends to canonical formulation of an entire dogmatic inventory of the Church. This is not to say that new dogmatic formulas are impossible in Orthodoxy, formulas which might be fixed by new ecumenical councils. But, strictly speaking, the minimum already existing constitutes a sufficient immovable base for the development of doctrine, without the disclosure of new dogmatic forms. This development manifests itself in the life of the Church, forming new lines of theological teaching ("theologoumena"). The predominance of "theologoumena" over dogmas is the special advantage of the Orthodox Church, which is a stranger to the legalistic spirit, even in the matter of doctrine. Orthodoxy has felt no disadvantage resulting from this impractical attitude, even when some diversity of theological opinions exists.

There is one fundamental Christian dogma, common to the entire Christian world, that is the dogma confessed by St. Peter in the name of all the Apostles and thus in the name of the Church:

"Thou are the Christ, the Son of the living God." This same dogma served as the subject for the preaching of the Apostles at the time of Pentecost. Jesus Christ is the eternal Word, the Son of God, Who has taken upon Himself human nature, without division or confusion, true God and true man, Who came into the world to save mankind, died on the Cross, rose again from the dead, ascended into heaven and is seated at the right hand of the Father, and Who will come again to this world for the Last Judgment and for His eternal reign. Concerning these articles of faith there is no difference whatever between Orthodoxy and the beliefs of Catholicism or those of Anglicanism—at least of Anglo-Catholicism—or those of orthodox Protestantism.

The Christological dogma is understood by Orthodoxy in all the power of the elaborate realism which it received in the time of the ecumenical councils. The expression of this dogma is finished and perfect for all time, although we now interpret it by applying to it the philosophical and theological categories of our present age. The idea of the love of God sacrificing itself for the fallen creature, love extending even to incarnation and to death on the Cross, and on the other hand the idea of the existence of the God-Man, the idea of a positive relation between God, Who created man in His image, and man, lifted by the incarnation to the possibility of deification—these two ideas are supreme evidences of a religious philosophy; they are expressed with an especial love in the Russian theological thought of our day. In any case, the prejudice according to which Orthodox Christology is "an extreme Hellenization of Christianity," is a theological naivete, born of rationalistic pride and shortsightedness. Orthodoxy is no less modern in its theology than is a "religions-geschichtliche Jesusism."

For Orthodoxy, faith in Christ, as Son of God, is not a Christological doctrine, but life itself. This faith penetrates life through and through. We throw ourselves at the feet of the Saviour with the joyful cry of faith: "My Lord and my God"; each of us is present at His nativity, suffers in His passion on the Cross, rises with Him, and awaits with fear His glorious return. Without that faith, there is hardly any Christianity, and in truth, those who try to make religion scientific, Christians without Christ, attain only one result; they have made Christianity, instead of a thing of spirit and of fire, something tiresome and mediocre. Christianity is faith in Christ, Son of God, Our Lord, Saviour and Redeemer: "The victory that overcomes the world, our faith"(1 John 5:4).

Faith in Christ, as Son of God, is also faith in the Holy Trinity, in whose name baptism is administered, according to the Christ's commandment (Matt. 28:19). The Trinitarian faith is already implied in faith in the Son, Who is sent by the Father and Who sends the Holy Spirit. Christianity is the religion of the Holy Trinity to such a degree that the concentration of piety on the Christ alone has become a deviation already known by a special term as "Jesusism." It should be noted that, in the liturgical life of Orthodoxy, in the exclamations, the doxologies, the prayers, the name of the Holy Trinity predominates over the name of Jesus, which shows that the knowledge of Christ is inseparably connected with that of the Holy Trinity. God is Spirit, Which has consciousness threefold and yet one, or equally a unity of life and of substance; and in that one-in-three, the special existence of three divine "hypostases" is reconciled with unity of self-consciousness. God is love. The Trinity possesses such a power of mutual love as to unite the three in one single life.

The dogma of the Holy Trinity is confessed by Orthodoxy in the form in which it was expressed at the time of the ecumenical councils and was fixed in the creed. Retaining these forms is not an archaism, for their supreme verity still imposes itself upon the religious and philosophical conscience of our time. This dogma is naturally incompatible with rationalism, which seeks to attain divine things by means of categories of unity and of plurality, but this does not make the Trinitarian dogma something foreign to theological reasoning. We find in our own consciences testimony so resplendent to the existence of the unity of the three "hypostases" (I—you—we) that this dogma becomes a necessity for thought and the point of departure of all metaphysics.[1] The dogma of the Holy Trinity is not only a doctrinal form, but a living Christian experience which is constantly developing; it is a fact of Christian life. For life in Christ unites with the Holy Trinity, gives a knowledge of the Father's love and the gifts of the Holy Spirit. There is no truly Christian life, apart from the knowledge of the Trinity; this is abundantly witnessed in Christian literature. Unitarianism is no longer Christianity and cannot be, and Orthodoxy can have nothing in common with it. As a matter of fact, recent Arianism, "Jesusism" and Unitarianism are allied and both are equally foreign to the Christianity of the Church.

The confession of faith in the Holy Trinity is a common bond for the whole Church, both before and after the separation. The chief difference between the Eastern Church and the Western, a difference which developed gradually, beginning from the fifth century, concerns the doctrine of the procession of the Holy Spirit. According to Orthodox teaching, the Father—the first principle, begets the Son before all ages (in the beginning), and from Him proceeds the Holy Spirit; it is a divine monarchy in the Holy Trinity. Here the question arises of the reciprocal relations between the second and the third "hypostases." According to patristic literature the Holy Spirit proceeds through the Son and rests on Him; such is the expression of their relationship in its origin. In the West that relation, which has never been made thoroughly clear in the Church, is understood as a participation of the Son in the procession of the Holy Spirit. Hence the theological discussions on the "filioque," brought about at first by a simple difference of theological opinion, which afterwards became a dogmatic disagreement, because a Western "theologoumenon" was made an indestructible dogma. The experience of the Conference of Bonn, between Orthodox and old Catholics, proves that it is possible, in spite of the past, to arrive at a mutual theological understanding on this point.

[1]See my *Chapters on the Trinity* (in Russian), *La Pensee Orthodoxe*, Paris, I., 1928, II, 1930, and *Die Tragodie der Philosophie*, Darmstadt, 1927, Leuchter Verlag.

God is the Creator of the World, which He created from the void. God does not seek to complete Himself by means of the world, but, in His goodness, He wishes non-being to share in being and to have His image reflected there. The creation of the world *ex nihilo* is the work of love, of almighty power and of divine wisdom. The creation is the work of the Holy Trinity. The Father creates by the Word in the Holy Spirit. The Holy Trinity is immediately directed towards the world by the Word, by means of which all things were made (John 1:3). The Son is the cosmic hypostasis who created, in announcing it, the ideal existence of the world. But the Holy Spirit also finishes, vivifies, gives to the world reality. The images of this world have their eternal foundations in God, and this eternal seed of being, plunged into non-being, produces the spiritual world, the angels (heaven) and the terrestrial world (the earth). The spiritual organism of these eternal prototypes of being constitutes the unique primordial principle of the world in God, the eternal wisdom which "the Lord created at the beginning of his work, the first of his acts of old" (Prov. 8:22,) and which was "beside him, like a master workman; and was daily his delight, rejoicing before him always" (Prov. 8:30), (cf. the books of the Wisdom of Solomon and the Wisdom of Joshua son of Sirach). The summit and the center of Creation is man: "I will take my delight (says Wisdom) in the sons of Men" (Prov. 8:31). Man is the end of creation; he is a microcosm, a world in little, and all the work of the six days may be understood as the gradual creation of man, created on the last day, to become the master of creation. The world of angels, so close to the throne of God, is certainly more highly placed from the hieratic point of view, but this is only a world of servitors, as compared to ours, where man is the head.[2]

Man is created in the image of God. In his personal consciousness man possesses the image of the divine hypostasis; as a member of the human race he possesses the image of the union of the three

---

[2]See my book, *Jacob's Ladder* (on the angels) in Russian, Paris, 1929.

hypostases. He is conscious of himself not only as I, but as you and as we. In masculine and feminine nature humanity possesses a double aspect of its spiritual existence, one aspect where reason predominates and another where beauty and love have chief place; these correspond to the figures of the second and the third hypostases. In possessing a body, man becomes not only a citizen of this world, but also its master; in him Divine Wisdom is realized, manifested in creation. This image of God revealed in man is the basis of both his creation and his destiny. But it must be realized in himself by himself, in liberty: this is his likeness to God.

The world and the first man issued from God's hand is innocent and perfect. But this was only a measure of created perfection which had to be confirmed by man's own free activity in the fulfilment of God's will and the attainment of his own perfection. The first man lived in a state of innocence; he was near to God and could even be in communion with Him. But man had to determine his future for himself, strengthened by God, thus reinforcing his own corporeal existence and raising it to immortality. The condition and the destiny of the world are bound up with those of man, who constitutes the center of that world. He received from God all that God could give him through His almighty power, but he could not and should not receive from God that which he was called to realize by his own free will; he is obliged, in a way, to create himself. This creation of himself in liberty is symbolically expressed by the teaching concerning the tree of good and evil. Man fell by disobeying the commandment; he committed what is called original sin. He permitted the egotistical element to predominate in him, he turned from God towards the world and he gave power to non-being from which he had been taken. He became carnal, mortal. His character as a creature limited, imperfect, manifests itself in all his life and leads him towards evil and error, in his mind, his will and his creative power. Man is isolated in the world, for his direct relations with God are ended. He is obliged to seek God, Who, before the fall, Himself came to converse with man. What has been the influence of original metaphysical sin on human nature?

Original sin means general corruption of human nature which has been diverted from its proper norm. Its first consequence was the loss of the state of Grace. Then came the general corruption of human nature, which, after it turned itself from life in God, became mortal. Our carnal nature ceased to obey the soul; on the contrary it began to have undue predominance; voluptuousness took possession of us. In our spiritual life appeared egoism, pride and jealousy, a true knowledge of good and evil, that is, of the constant struggle between light and darkness.

Thus human liberty became restricted; man was made the slave of his nature, captive of his flesh and passions. Nevertheless, all this perversion of our true nature could not completely paralyse and enfeeble human liberty. The person remained a person, a free spiritual being, who, aided by the special help of God, is capable and worthy of deification, capable and worthy of Incarnation.

Man, created in the image of God, destined, in realizing his divine resemblance, to be made like God, had strayed from the way. But God Himself, Who imprinted on man His own image, became man. He was born of the Holy Spirit and of the Virgin Mary, by His conception escaping the taint of sin. He united in His hypostasis divine and human nature. He became the man Jesus. He took upon Himself all humanity, becoming the new Adam, universal man, and all His works are thus of universal value. He made His human will conformable with that of God and thus raised his humanity to the height of immortality. In His spiritual suffering—the Garden of Gethsemane, in His corporeal suffering—the death on the Cross, He bore all the weight of human sin and of men's rejection by God. He offered to the God of justice a sacrifice of propitiation. He redeemed us from our sin and reconciled us with God. Through Him, divine nature reclothed human nature, without destroying it, as fire reddens iron. He gave to salvation, life eternal in God, even here among afflictions, and participation in the future life, for, risen Himself, He will raise up in the flesh all humanity.

The salvation of all is, then, the deification of human nature. Individual salvation is the appropriation of this gift by a personal effort, for deification is not a physical or magical act on a person, but an interior action, a work of grace, in the person. This work is accomplished with the cooperation of human liberty and not without will. It is life in Christ, under the guidance of the Holy Spirit. Our effort is joined mysteriously to the gift of God, by this capacity for deification. The whole person must be engaged in this effort. He must strive to become God-like through the action of faith, which testifies of his redemption by the blood of Christ and his reconciliation with God. But the striving for salvation is also expressed by works, which are the natural fruit of faith and constitute at the same time the way, the life of faith: "Faith without works is dead." Faith and its works: this is our share in our deification through the power of Christ, this is the realization of our likeness to God, of the image of God restored in us, the image which is the Christ.

Here there is no place for the idea of merit of any sort—supererogatory or not—by which man might acquire the full right to the gift of grace, for grace is incommensurable with any merit, whatever it may be, and remains a pure gift, a free gift "gratia gratis data." Good works do not constitute merit—no one merits or can merit salvation by human works. They represent man's personal participation in achieving salvation, beyond any reckoning or compensation. The capacity for deification, for becoming God-like, is without limit, like eternity. This is why the idea of works of supererogation or of merit is just as erroneous as that other extreme, according to which man has no part in the realization of his salvation, under the pretext that the latter is already accomplished for us by God, and that it is sufficient to learn this by an act of faith. Nevertheless, if we subtract from this Protestant idea, of salvation by faith without works, its onesidedness, which is a natural reaction against the Catholic arithmetic of merit, we can understand it in a more profound sense. In this more profound conception, faith is not an instantaneous act, but an enduring state which is constantly reaffirmed; and to be affirmed, faith should be active; it must include good works.

In this interpretation the Protestant idea of salvation by active faith is nearer the Orthodox conception than the Catholic doctrine of merit, in so far as the latter idea rejects all sense of equivalence between faith and salvation. But this idea becomes one-sided when it denies our participation in our own salvation, thus denying to us all liberty, because of our fallen nature and original sin. This onesidedness produces the idea that may be forgiven and justified by faith alone, since we are incapable of anything else. And faith is then only our act of beholding our own salvation. But we have preserved a residuum of our primitive liberty, and cannot lose it without losing the image of God and the spirituality of our being. Consequently, we are called upon to achieve in ourselves our own salvation. The individual forms, the ways and the different degrees of this salvation are capable of development, but in any case we must participate personally in our salvation. By so doing we do not become our own co-redeemer and co-saviour with Christ, but we are active in the appropriation of our salvation, we seek it personally, we labor at it during all our life. In this sense, individual salvation, personal effort (''works'') may be called merit, and the salvation attained, recompense. In the relative sense I have indicated, it may then be said that we deserve our portion in eternal beatitude. But this has nothing in common with the pharisaical and juridical idea that one can save oneself by good works.

In general the juridical idea plays only a minor part in the Orthodox idea of salvation, while in other confessions it occupies a much larger place. Without minimizing the idea of divine justice, which must be satisfied, Orthodoxy considers that the love of God forms the center of the doctrine of salvation. For God so loved the world that He spared not His Son to save and deify it. The Incarnation, first decreed to ransom fallen humanity and reconcile it with God, is understood by Orthodoxy as, above all, the deification of man, as the communication of the divine life to him. To fallen man the Incarnation became the supreme way for his reconciliation with God, the way of redemption. This produces the concept of salvation as deification. The redemption is the voluntary sacrifice of Christ, Who took upon Himself, together with our nature, our sin as well.

That is the mystery of the Redemption where the One intercedes for all humanity. But in Orthodoxy the idea of divine Justice is deeply joined with that of the Love of God for man, a gracious and pitying love which leads to salvation. Redemption by the Incarnation is not only our liberation from sin by the sacrifice of the Saviour, it is also a new creation, a definitive creation of the person as God, not according to nature, but according to grace, creation not by the omnipotence of God, as in the beginning, but by His sacrificing love. Christ, in His holy and sinless humanity, sanctified and deified all human nature.

But this salvation of human beings, effectuated by Christ, the new Adam, in a free act, for all humanity—this salvation must be freely accepted by each particular person. God realizes the objective aspect and lays the foundation for our salvation, but we must realize the subjective side and choose salvation. It is not enough, then, for us to believe passively that we are saved, for that faith leaves us conscious of our impotence and gives us the certitude of being justified before the judgment of God only by a legal fiction, by the application of a sort of amnesty. And no more can we merit salvation by our own efforts (faith and works), salvation being conferred on us by the love of God. Nor can we multiply this gift, founding the claim on a right which belongs to us, but we can and we should appropriate for ourselves the immense gift of deification, according to the degree of our own, creating in ourselves resemblance to God of which the unique foundation is Christ.

CHAPTER 7

THE SACRAMENTS

The Holy Spirit which abides in the Church communicates its gifts, to each member according to our needs. The life of Grace is accomplished in the Church, for each member, in its own special ways, mysterious and unfathomable. Nevertheless Our Lord has been pleased to establish a definite way, accessible to all, for the reception of the Grace of the Holy Spirit, in the holy mysteries. The mysteries (sacraments) are sacred acts, when, under a visible sign, there is conferred a definite, invisible gift of the Holy Spirit.

The essential of the sacraments is a union of things visible and invisible, of an exterior form with an interior content. The very nature of the Church is here reflected, of that Church which is the invisible in the visible, and the visible in the invisible. The divine institution of the sacraments establishes order, measure and law in the domain of spiritual life. It imposes limits to the disordered, unformed, hysterical ecstasy which characterizes the mystic sects such as the "Holy Rollers" or the Russian "Scourgers"; it gives a divine, objective foundation to the life of Grace.

In the sacraments the Holy Spirit is conferred, always and unchangeably, in a manner regulated by the Church, but it is received differently by different people. The Church has the power to invoke the Holy Spirit in the sacraments. Pentecost, which happened in the past for the assembled apostles, is always happening in the heart of the Church in the sacraments, thanks to the apostolic succession of the hierarchy. This is why the power to administer the sacraments is vitally connected with the priesthood. Where there is no priest there are no sacraments (baptism excepted). This does not mean that, in such cases, the Holy Spirit is absent, for the way of the sacraments is not the only one which gives the Holy Spirit. The Spirit breathes where it wills, and its gift of the Holy Spirit is not confined to the sacraments, even in the Church. The gift of the

Holy Spirit does not depend on human cognizance: no one knows whence it comes or whither it goes. In the sacraments of the Church, on the other hand, there is found a knowledge of, and a definite form for the giving of the Holy Spirit. The Church possesses true sacraments, active sacraments—this is one of the signs of the true Church.

At first glance it may seem that the seven sacraments of Catholicism coincide with those of Orthodoxy: baptism, chrismation (confirmation), penitence, the eucharist, the laying on of hands, marriage, an ointment for the sick. But is the coincidence perfect? This doctrine of the ''seven sacraments'' has recently acquired the force of a dogmatic tradition in the Church. But it was formed only in the beginning of the twelfth century, first in the West and later in the East. It must be remembered that the number seven has no conclusive meaning, for the number of sacramentals (''sacramentalia'') in the Church is much larger. There are, for example, special forms of many blessings (of a church, of holy water, especially at Epiphany, then of bread, fruit, all objects); even funerals and monastic vows were once formally called sacraments. All these rites as well as many others, such as the consecration of crosses and icons, do not differ from the ''seven sacraments'' in what concerns their active force, for they also confer the grace of the Holy Spirit, when certain exterior forms are observed. The ''seven sacraments'' are only the most important manifestations of the sacramental power inherent in the Church.

At the same time there is no reason why we should not distinguish, even among the seven sacraments, different degrees in their universal character and even as to their divine institution, although all the sacraments are equally mysterious, since they confer the gifts of the Holy Spirit. But the Orthodox, together with Protestants, can set apart from the rest Baptism and the Eucharist as instituted by Our Lord Himself and as being indispensable for all Christians. These are the ''evangelical sacraments.'' They have existed from the very beginning of the life of the Church. The other sacraments are also founded on the words of Scripture, and, directly

or indirectly, on the words of Our Lord, but they were only gradually established by the Church. Certain among them (for example,
marriage, holy orders, anointment) are not administered to all
members of the Church. Such distinctions, however, belong more
to the domain of theology than to that of practical life. In practice, it
is the priesthood which serves as basis for all the sacraments, baptism excepted. But the priest was constituted only in the post-
apostolic period, when someone had to replace the apostles departed
from this world, and something had to replace primitive charismatism.

Taken together, the seven sacraments sanctify the life of man and
assure him plenitude of grace. A special power is inherent in each
sacrament.

(1) Baptism is a spiritual birth. In putting on Christ the natural
man dies, together with the original sin innate in him. A new person is engendered. It is the appropriation of the saving power of the
redemptive work of Christ. Baptism is the only sacrament which, in
the absence of a priest, may be administered by the layman (man or
woman) by virtue of the universal Christian priesthood. But it can
be administered only by a Christian and by the power of the
Church, whose instrument the Christian is; baptism administered
by a non-Christian, Roman Catholic ideas to the contrary notwithstanding, would not be valid, for it is an act of the grace of the
Church and not an act of magic. The form for baptism is a triple im-
mersion in the name of the Holy Trinity. All Christian baptism
conferred in the name of the Holy Trinity is valid, not only within
Orthodoxy, but outside its limits; the practice of the Church, ancient and modern, is sufficient testimony to this. As a general rule
those who have been baptized once are not re-baptized, save in exceptional circumstances.

(2) Chrismation (confirmation) is administered in the Orthodox
Church immediately after baptism. It cannot be administered by a
layman, but only by a priest or a bishop, and the holy chrism used
for this sacrament is blessed by an assembly of bishops, so that it is
an episcopal sacrament, although immediately administered by a

priest. This sacrament is the substitute for the laying on of hands by the Apostles. In the primitive Church the Apostles laid their hands on all those who were baptized, conferring on them not an hieratic dignity but the sacred title of Christian (layman). This is why episcopal authority confers it now. Through this sacrament the Christian has access to the life of grace in the Church by means of participation in all the other sacraments. Christians who unite themselves to Orthodoxy after being members of confessions deprived of a recognized priesthood, are joined to the Church by Chrismation. It is only after Chrismation that they can partake of the other sacraments. Chrismation, during which the chrism is administered with the words, "The 'seal' of gift of the Holy Spirit," corresponds to an individual Pentecost in the life of each Christian. Each Christian receives the gift of the Holy Spirit which is proper to him; he receives anew the glory inherent in the soul and body of the first Adam, lost after the fall (Rom 3:23), the germ of the transfiguration and the resurrection.

(3) Penitence, sometimes called second baptism, is the application of the power to "retain or to remit" sins, given by Christ to the Apostles and their successors. Although, at baptism, the domination of original sin is abolished in man, nevertheless the power of sin remains in his natural being in the form of the inclination to sin and of general evil. To free himself from sin committed after baptism, man confesses his faults to an authorized minister, bishop or priest; the latter gives absolution which confers grace, wipes out the sins and reconciles man to God.

(4) The Eucharist or Lord's Supper is the reception of heavenly food in the Communion of the Body and Blood of Christ, according to the institution of our Lord Himself. This sacrament can be administered only by a legally instituted priest or bishop. The Church teaches that the bread and wine are changed into the Body and Blood of Christ, given in the Holy Supper. But Orthodoxy does not agree with the Latin doctrine of transubstantiation that distinguishes the substance, which changes, from the accidents, which do not change.[1] Christ, Who is offered in the mystery of the Holy

[1]See my article: "Eucharistic Dogma," in Russian, La Voie, 1930, Nos. 1 and 2.

Supper, is truly there present. In Orthodoxy the Holy Gifts are used only for Communion. Orthodoxy does not practise the cult of the consecrated elements outside the liturgy: the exposition of the Host, Benediction given with it, or Adoration of the Reserved Host, as among Catholics. The sanctification of the Holy Gifts operates during all the liturgy, whose essential part consists in the words of institution of Our Lord following the invocation of the Holy Spirit, ("epiklesis") and the benediction of the elements. All the faithful, that is, not only the clergy but the laity also, communicate under two species. The Eucharist is the oblation of the bloodless sacrifice and has the power of the sacrifice of Golgotha; it is a sharing in that sacrifice. It is offered "for all and for everything," for the living and the dead.

(5) The laying on of hands (Holy Orders) is a sacrament where hieratic gifts are conferred by the bishop who places his hands on the head of the recipient. The people of the Church consent to this ordination; they participate in it by will, word and prayer. The grace conferred by this sacrament is ineffaceable and Holy Orders may never be repeated (although unworthy clerics may be forbidden to exercise their function). There are three hieratic degrees: the bishopric, the priesthood, and the diaconate. Inferior orders, such as reader and sub-deacon, are not included in the hierarchy instituted by the imposition of hands.

(6) Marriage is a sanctification of the natural union of man and woman for a Christian life together and for procreation. Marriage, which is consummated "in Christ and in the Church," lays the foundation for a domestic church, the family.

(7) Anointing of the sick is the sacrament of the restoration to health of the whole human being, body and soul. Release from sin as a result of penitence and aid in the struggle against sinfulness are joined to physical healing. Anointing may bring either return to health or the increase of spiritual strength necessary to a Christian death; hence this sacrament has two faces; one turns toward healing, the other toward the liberation from illness by death. In Catholicism this sacrament has only the latter significance, the

preparation for death.

Beside these seven sacraments, the Church's life of grace includes many acts of sanctification and many rites which possess sacramental power (''sacramentalia''). It may be said that all the acts of the Church service are of this sort. We shall not stop to study these. Let us say only that by their means, through earthly matter and under divers forms, the grace of the Holy Spirit is constantly diffused upon the world. This grace is preparing the cosmos for its future transfiguration, for the creation of a new heaven and a new earth. The help of grace is offered to man according to his personal needs, by benediction, by prayer and by church services. The power which sanctifies and makes operative is the name of God. Blessing and sanctification are given in the name of God. Hence, in Orthodoxy, this name is accorded special veneration, which corresponds to that accorded to the name of God (the sacred tetragram) in the Old Testament. The sweetest among names, the name of Our Lord Jesus, is constantly repeated in the ''prayer of Jesus,'' a form of continuous, inner, silent prayer, peculiar to Orthodoxy. Veneration of the name of God is the foundation of Orthodox piety and liturgy.[1]

---

[1] See my book: *Introduction philosophique à la vénération du nom de Dieu* (in Russian), 1953.

CHAPTER 8

THE VIRGIN AND THE SAINTS IN ORTHODOXY

The Orthodox Church venerates the Virgin Mary as "more honorable than the cherubin and beyond compare more glorious than the seraphim," as superior to all created beings. The Church sees in her the Mother of God, who, without being a substitute for the One Mediator, intercedes before her Son for all humanity. We ceaselessly pray to her to intercede for us. Love and veneration for the Virgin is the soul of Orthodox piety, its heart, that which warms and animates its entire body. A faith in Christ which does not include His virgin birth and the veneration of His Mother is another faith, another Christianity from that of the Orthodox Church. Protestantism is this other sort of Christianity, with its strange and deeply-rooted lack of feeling for the Mother of God, a condition which dates from the Reformation. In this lack of veneration for the Virgin, Protestantism differs in almost equal measure from both Orthodoxy and Catholicism. Hence even the Protestant comprehension of the Incarnation loses some of its fulness and power.

The perfect union of divine and human in Christ is directly connected with the sanctification and the glorification of human nature, that is, above all, with the Mother of God. Without this concept the Incarnation becomes only something external, kenotic, a voluntary self-humiliation by the assumption of human nature, as the price necessary to purchase the justification of humanity before God. Here the Incarnation is only a means of Redemption, become a bitter necessity because of sin—and hence the Virgin Mary is only an instrument for the Incarnation, inevitable, but still something external, an instrument which is laid aside and forgotten when the need has passed. This forgetfulness of the Virgin Mary is often found in Protestantism even in such extreme beliefs as that the Virgin might have other children by Joseph, or even a denial of the virgin birth itself. The Church never separates Mother and Son, she who was incarnated by Him who was incarnate. In adoring the humanity of Christ, we venerate His Mother, from whom He received that humanity and who, in her person, represents the whole of humanity. Through the grace of God, in her all the sanctity accessible to humanity is attained, even after the fall, in the Church of the Old Testament. Thus the Church of the Old Testament had for its purpose the elevation, the conservation and the preparation of a holy humanity worthy to receive the Holy Spirit, that is, worthy of the Annunciation, in the person of the Virgin. Hence Mary is not merely the instrument, but the direct positive condition of the Incarnation, its human aspect. Christ could not have been incarnate by some mechanical process, violating human nature. It was necessary for that nature itself to say for itself, by the mouth of the most pure human being: ''Behold the handmaid of the Lord, be it unto me according to Thy word.'' At that moment the Holy Spirit descended upon her; the Annunciation was the Pentecost of the Virgin, and the Spirit completely sanctified and abode with her.

The Orthodox Church does not accept the Catholic dogma of 1854—the dogma of the Immaculate Conception of the Virgin, in the sense that she was exempt at birth from original sin. This would separate her from the human race, and she would then have been unable to transmit to her Son this true humanity.[1] But Orthodoxy does not admit in the All-pure Virgin any individual sin, for that would be unworthy of the dignity of the Mother of God. The connection between the Virgin and her Son does not cease with His birth. It continues in the same degree that the divine and human are inseparably united in Christ. During the earthly ministry of Our Lord the Virgin, infinitely humble, remains in the background. She leaves it only to take her place near the Cross of Golgotha with Him; she shared His Passion. She was also the first to participate in His Resurrection. The Virgin Mary is the center, invisible but real, of the Apostolic Church; it is in her that the secret of primitive Christianity is hidden, as well as that of the Evangel of the Spirit, written by St. John, whom Christ gave her for a son, as He hung

[1]See my book: *The Unburned Bush*, on the Orthodox cult of the Virgin; in Russian, Paris, 1927.

upon the Cross. The Church believes that, dying a natural death, she was not subject to corruption, but, raised up by her Son, she lives in her glorified body at the right hand of Christ in the heavens. In her is realized the idea of Divine Wisdom in the creation of the world, and Divine Wisdom in the created world. It is in her that Divine Wisdom is justified, and thus the veneration of the Virgin blends with that of the Holy Wisdom. In the Virgin there are united Holy Wisdom and the Wisdom of the created world, the Holy Spirit and the human hypostasis. Her body is completely spiritual and transfigured. She is the justification, the end and the meaning of creation. She is, in this sense, the glory of the world. In her God is already "all in all."

Living in heaven in a state of glory the Virgin remains the mother of the human race for which she prays and intercedes. This is why the Church addresses to her its supplications, invoking her aid. She covers the world with her veil praying, weeping for the sins of the world; at the Last Judgment she will intercede before her Son and ask pardon from Him. She sanctifies the whole natural world; in her and by her the world attains transfiguration. In a word, the veneration of the Virgin marks with its imprint all Christian anthropology and cosmology and all the life of prayer and piety.

Prayers addressed to the Virgin occupy a large place in the Orthodox service. Besides the feasts and the days specially consecrated to her, every office contains innumerable prayers addressed to her and her name is constantly spoken in the temple together with the name of Our Lord Jesus Christ. Her icons are found before us on the iconostasis and in different places in the church and in the houses of the faithful. There exist numerous types of these icons, the originals of which are considered as miraculous. This warmth natural to the cult of the Virgin comes from her humanity and her feminine nature. I sometimes think that the coldness of atmosphere of some Protestant churches results from the absence of just this warmth. In her and by her the feminine receives a place in piety, in connection with the Holy Spirit. The deep veneration of the Virgin in Orthodoxy sometimes shocks outside observers because it seems analogous with paganism. Such critics discover the prototype of the Virgin in Isis and other female divinities. But even if it were admitted that paganism had a certain obscure prescience, the difference between these goddesses and the Virgin, who is a glorified creature, completely deified, is too evident to warrant any comparison. It must be remarked that the nuances which characterize the cult of the Virgin in the West (the chivalric cult of the Madonna, of the ''belle dame'') are entirely unknown to the sober spirit of Orthodoxy which rejects the least hint of eroticism.

The cult of the Saints occupies a considerable place in Orthodox piety. The Saints are our intercessors and our protectors in the heavens and, in consequence, living and active members of the Church militant. Their blessed presence in the Church manifests itself in their pictures and their relics. They surround us with a cloud of prayer, a cloud of the glory of God. This cloud of witnesses does not separate us from Christ, but brings us nearer, unites us to Him. The Saints are not mediators between God and man—this would set aside the Unique Mediator, which is Christ—but they are our friends, who pray with us, and aid us in our Christian ministry and in our communion with Christ. Sometimes veneration of saints is seen as approaching the pagan cult of heroes or demigods, even to be equivalent to pagan polytheism. The parallel is not at all as deceptive as it seems, however. Paganism, with all its superstitions and delusions, could contain important premonitions, ''foreshadowings,'' which for reasons of divine pedagogy and to construct the Old Testament church, could remain unknown even to it. This may be the case of veneration for ''demi-gods,'' who are truly gods by grace, who were known to the pagan world but unknown to Old Testament Judaism. It would have been a temptation beyond its strength for Judaism to diverge toward polytheism from the strict monotheism in which the chosen people were nurtured. Only after the coming of Christ could the unbridgeable chasm, as well as the closeness, between Christ and ''those who belong to Jesus Christ'' (Gal. 5:24) become clear. The dogmatic basis for the veneration of saints lies precisely in this link. The

Church is the Body of Christ and those who are saved in the Church receive the power and the life of Christ, they are deified. They become "gods by virtue of grace"; they become christs in Jesus Christ.

Although man's lot will be decided finally at the Last Judgment of Christ, already at the so-called preliminary judgment, which takes place after the death for each person, the designation for glory and a crown of holiness becomes clear. It glows on the brow of a godly person even in his lifetime, for the judgment is only an open confirmation of his real state. "Life eternal" in God begins yet here, in the flux of time, which has the profundity of eternity, but on departure from this life it becomes the defining principle of existence.

Orthodoxy does not believe that the glorification of the Saints is founded on the special merits of the Saints before God—merits supererogatory or necessary—a recompense which they have received, and which they can in turn use for the benefit of those who have not sufficient merit. That proud conception would truly put the Saints in the rank of demi-gods. The Saints are those who by their active faith and love have become like God, and show forth the image of God in its power, those who have obtained for themselves abundant grace. In this purification of the heart by an heroic effort of mind and body lies the road to salvation for every man in which Christ abides: "It is no longer I who live, but Christ who lives in me" (Gal. 2:20). In the words of the Lord: "If a man loves me, he will keep my word, and my Father will love him, and we will come to him and make our home with him" (Jn. 14:23). On this road to salvation there are quantitative distinctions between persons which become qualitative and decisive for one's eternal fate. Beyond this threshold our salvation is accomplished as a decisive self-determination, and then begins the growth in grace, corresponding for each of us to our personal image and the type of our spiritual personality. Sanctity has as many forms as there are human individualities. The sublime work of holiness always has an individual and creative character. The Church knows divers degrees of sanctity or spiritual aspects of salvation: prophets, apostles, martyrs, doctors, venerable monks, soldiers and kings. And certainly this list is not complete: each epoch (ours among them) reveals new aspects of holiness, in addition to those already existing. Besides, not all the Saints are known to the world; there are those whom Our Lord permits to remain unknown to us. There is a feast of All Saints where all the Saints together are commemorated, both those who are glorified and those who are not.

Saints can help us, not by force of their deserts but by force of the spiritual freedom in love that they have acquired through their spiritual efforts. This freedom gives them the power to represent us before God in prayer, and also in effective love for human beings. God accords to the Saints, as to the angels, the power to accomplish His will by active though invisible aid accorded to men. They are the Church "invisible" which lives with the same life as the Church visible. They are the hands of God by which God performs his works. This is why it is given to the Saints to do deeds of love even after their death, not as works necessary to their salvation—for their salvation is already attained—but to aid their brothers in the way of salvation.

The extent of the power of the Saints' effective participation corresponds to the extent of their spirit and to the magnitude of their efforts, "for star differs from star in glory" (1 Cor. 15:41). While there are degrees in sanctity, the members of the human race subject to original sin, of course, cannot have levels of distinction comparable to the great and saving power of Christ's redemptive sacrifice. Even the Pure Virgin bears witness to "God My Saviour" (Lk 1:47). But our incomparability in this respect certainly does not remove distinctions in the forms of acquiring even natural human gifts which are granted to them (ability for learning, for art, for practical skills, etc.), this is all the more true of spiritual life. Spiritual effort is a creative endeavor to acquire the Holy Spirit. It is achieved by becoming free from sin, which is granted to us by mastering a redemptive sacrifice. If we were passively indifferent to this effort, the division into sheep and goats at the Day of Judgment would not take place. Judgement presupposes distinctions in the achievement of sanctity.

The existence of the Saints in the Church is not only possible, but necessary for us. Each soul must have its own direct contact with Christ, its own conversation with Him, its own life in the Saviour. And in this there cannot be any mediator, just as there is none in our participation in the Eucharist: each person receives the Body and Blood of the Lord and is mystically joined with Him. But the soul which clings individually to Christ should not be isolated. The sons of men, who belong to the same human race, cannot and should not be shut up in isolation. And before the Christ Who taught us to say ''Our Father'' we find ourselves together, with all our brothers, either those who are here with us on earth or those who are already with the Saints. This is ''the communion of Saints.'' We are conscious, at one time, both of the immediate nearness and dearness of Christ and of the presence of our Lord and Judge. It is naturally necessary to hide ourselves in awe before the Judge of all, and here we take refuge beneath the protection of the Virgin and the Saints. For they belong to our race and kind. With them we may speak in our language of human frailty, and thus, in mutual comprehension, stand shoulder to shoulder with them before the terrrible judgment seat of God.

Of course, in our prayers, addressed to the Saints, a certain interior, spiritual perspective must be observed. The Saints should not veil for us the grandeur of Christ; and our life in Christ, and through Him in the Holy Trinity, should not be diminished. The conscience of the Church shows us the right degree to maintain. But it cannot be denied that in practice, superstition and the lack of religious teaching can bring us near to polytheism and near a ''syncretism'' where pagan vestiges exist tranquilly, side by side with Christianity. But this is not due to the cult of the Saints in itself. Those who reject this cult suffer great spiritual loss; while remaining near to Christ, they lose their true relation to Him. They are destined to remain spiritually without a family, without race, without home, without fathers and brothers in Christ. They traverse the way of salvation all alone, each one for himself without looking for examples and without knowing communion with others. Certainly all this is not accomplished without a vigorous logic, and the authority and example of the Saints of the Church are replaced by the teaching of the doctors (for example, the apostles). But from these latter only teaching is received; it is impossible to pray with them or to them, for prayer, to be in common with those no longer with us, must be addressed to them.

How does the Church learn the mystery of the Judgment of God about the Saints? In other words, how is the glorification of the Saints attained? Speaking generally, the answer to this question is as follows: this glorification becomes self-evident to the Church. Special signs, different in each case, miracles, the incorruptibility of relics, and above all, evident spiritual aid testify to them. By an official act of canonization the Church authorities only testify to facts already evident to the ecumenical conscience of the Church, and make legal the veneration of a given Saint. As a matter of fact, this glorification (local or general) always precedes the juridical canonization which confirms it. In Orthodoxy, the act of canonization does not call for so meticulous a procedure as in Catholicism. Canonization is effected by an act of ecclesiastical authority—ecumenical or local. The source of sanctity is never exhausted in the Church, which has known Saints in all times of its existence. And doubtless the future will manifest new aspects of sanctity, each conformable to the life of its epoch.

One consequence of the cult of the Saints is the veneration of their relics. Sometimes bodily incorruption is even revered as a sign of sanctity. Incorruption, however, is by no means a general rule, and it is not all essential for a saint to be canonized. The relics of the Saints, when they are preserved, are very specially venerated. To indicate a particular instance, portions of relics are placed in the "antimension," the silken napkin on which the liturgy is celebrated. This is in remembrance of the primitive Church, where the liturgy was celebrated on the tombs of the martyrs. From the dogmatic point of view, the veneration of relics (as well as that of the icons of Saints) is founded on faith in a special connection between the spirit of the Saint and his human remains, a connection which death does not destroy. In the case of the Saints the power of death is limited; their souls do not altogether leave their bodies, but remain present in spirit and in grace in their relics, even in the smallest portion. The relics are bodies already glorified in earnest of the general resurrection, although still awaiting that event. They have the same nature as that of the body of Christ in the tomb, which, although it was dead and awaiting its resurrection, deserted by the soul, still was not altogether abandoned by His divine spirit.

Each day of the ecclesiastical year is consecrated to the memory of a Saint or Saints. The lives of the Saints are an inestimable source of Christian edification in the Eastern Church, as well as in that of the West. The Church never lacks Saints, any more than it lacks the grace of the Holy Spirit, love and faith. "The golden crown" of Saints, known and unknown to the world, will continue to the end of time. The last great Saint glorified in the Russian Church in the twentieth century is the venerable Seraphim of Sarov. He radiated the joy of the Holy Spirit. His greeting to visitors was always: "Joy, Christ is risen!" There are many servitors of the Church and many ascetics of the nineteenth century whom the faithful consider as Saints, but who are not yet formally canonized—since this is impossible owing to the present persecution in Russia. This is the case with many "startsi," spiritual guides of monks and of the people, among others those of the monastery of Optina and of other monasteries. It is the case with bishops like Theophan the Recluse (†1894), who remained thirty years in complete seclusion in the convent of Vyshensky. This is the case with priests like Father John of Kronstadt. As to martyrs, Russia of our day counts them by thousands. They are "the souls of those who were beheaded for having testified to Jesus and for having believed in the word of God, and the souls of those who have not worshipped the beast" (Rev.20:4).

First among all the Saints, nearest to the throne of God, is St. John the Baptist, "the friend of the Bridegroom," the greatest among those born of woman. This closeness evolves, first of all, from the significance granted to the Baptist at Epiphany and the descent of the Holy Spirit upon the Baptized. It was like a second spiritual birth from the Holy Spirit. It also comes from the special ministry of John the Forerunner himself, whose whole life was devoted to preparing the way for the Other, demonstrating an incomparable spiritual effort of self-denial. "He must increase, but I must decrease" (Jn. 3:30). He was called to reveal the Messiah to the world: "Behold the Lamb of God, who has taken the sins of the world," and then, withdrawing into dark shadow, to accept a martyr's death of beheading. Before this he bears witness and is glorified by his friend. Of him Jesus said, "Yet wisdom is justified by her deeds" (Matt. 11:19). This means that John has achieved the supreme human sanctity and the purpose of creation. The wisdom which was with God at the creation of the world and whose joy is in the sons of men is justified in John, and still more justified in the Virgin Mary. Both of them, the Theotokos and the Forerunner, together present to the Word Incarnate the pinnacle and glory of creation, the closest to the angelic world. This belief is expressed iconographically in the "Deisis," a group depicting the Saviour enthroned, with the Virgin and the Forerunner at His right and left hand. This indicates that the Baptist shares with the Mother of God a special nearness to Christ; hence he shares, as well, her special approach to Christ in prayer. The Virgin and the Precursor stand together before the Incarnate Word as representing the summit and the glory of creation; they are nearer to Him than the world of angels. The same idea is expressed in the arrangement of icons on the iconostasis (a screen which hides the sanctuary in Orthodox churches). The icons of Christ, flanked by those of the Virgin and the Precursor, occupy a central place; afterwards come those of angels and of other Saints. The Virgin, it is true, is glorified by the Church as being "more honourable than the cherubim and beyond compare more glorious than the seraphim." But the Precursor is also placed higher than the world of angels. Iconography sometimes expresses this by representing the Precursor with wings, like an angel (see Mal. 3:1 and Matt. 11:10). His superhuman, angelic ministry is combined with perfect human sanctity, and by this union he acquires primacy in the angelic world as well, where he is sometimes assigned the place occupied by the Morning Star before the Fall. Also among the Saints, "the friends of God," the friend of the Bridegroom has primacy, giving way only to the Theotokos, together with whom he represents the human race in prayer before God.

The Saints in their totality, headed by the Theotokos and the Forerunner, form the glory of God in human creation. Wisdom is justified in them. This thought is expressed in the verse which forms the prokeimenon in the service of the saints: "God is wonderful in his saints, the God of Israel." "God has taken his place in the divine council; in the midst of the gods he holds judgment" (Ps. 82:1). The created glory, "the divine council," the crown of creation, corresponds to the Glory of God before the ages.

The glory of God's creation consists not only in the world of men but also in that of angels, not only in "the world," but also in "heaven." The Orthodox Church has a doctrine concerning the angels, and in practice the veneration of angels approaches that of the Saints. Like the Saints, angels pray and intercede for the human race and we address our prayers to them. But this rapprochement does not wipe out the difference that exists between the world of incorporeal powers in the human race. Angels form a special domain of creation, which is nevertheless allied to humanity.[1] Angels, like men, are formed in the image of God. But the plenitude of that image is inherent only in man; possessing a body he participates in the whole terrestrial world and rules over it, according to the divine law. The angels, on the contrary, having no body, have no world and no nature belonging especially to them; but they are always near God and live always in Him. The angels are spiritual essences. It is said sometimes that they have transparent bodies, sometimes also—and this corresponds better with the fundamentals—that they have no bodies at all. Nevertheless, even without bodies, the holy

[1] See my book: *Jacob's Ladder: On the Angels*, (in Russian), Paris, 1929.

angels are in a positive relation with the world of humanity

The Church teaches that each man has a guardian angel who stands before the face of the Lord. This guardian angel is not only a friend and a protector, who preserves from evil and who sends good thought; the image of God is reflected in the creature—angels and men—in such a way that angels are celestial prototypes of men. Guardian angels are especially our spiritual kin. Scripture testified that the guardianship and direction of the elements, of places, of peoples, of societies, are confided to the guardian angels of the cosmos, whose very substance adds something of harmony to the elements they watch over. According to the testimony of Revelation, the angels share, constantly and actively, in the life of the world, as well as in the life of each one of us; by becoming attuned to the spiritual life we can hear these voices of the world beyond and feel that we are in touch with them. The world of angels, which we know at our birth and which is therefore accessible to our remembrance (anamnesis of Plato), opens to us on the threshold of death, where—according to the belief of the Church—the angels greet and guide the soul of the departed.

But side by side with the angels of light there are fallen angels or demons, evil spirits, who strive to influence us, acting upon our sinful inclinations. Evil spirits become visible to those who have attained a certain degree of spiritual experience. The Gospels and the whole of the New Testament give us unshakable testimony on this point. Orthodoxy understands this testimony in a manner wholly realistic; it does not accept an allegorical exegesis and even less refuses to explain these texts by the simple influence of religious syncretism. The spiritual world and the existence of good and evil spirits are evident to all those who live the spiritual life. And the belief in the holy angels is a great joy and a consolation for the Christian. The Orthodox pray to their guardian angels and all the celestial powers, above all to the archangels Michael and Gabriel.

According to Orthodox usage, at baptism a name is given in honor of a Saint who is later known as the angel of the given Christian. The day of his memory is called ''the day of his angel.'' This suggests that the Saint and the guardian angel are so conjoined, in the service of a given person, that they are called by the same name (although they are not identical). Following a spiritual change, such as the taking of monastic vows, which is, one might say, a new birth, the name is changed; this is the case with the entry into religion, and he who bears a new name is henceforth confided to a new Saint. The veneration of holy angels and Saints creates in Orthodoxy a spiritual family atmosphere, full of love and repose. This veneration cannot be separated from the love of Christ and the Church—His Body.

But the dark spirits, fallen angels, enter into the realm of light; their influence corrupts the life of men. Against these spirits, heaven and men and the spiritual world wage a battle in the spirit. These evil powers in men add to their weakness and sometimes engage in direct and open warfare (the life of the great ascetics and anchorites testifies to this). The Church is not far from the demonology professed by the Gospel and the whole of the New Testament. Certainly these conceptions are now complicated by the facts that science reveals to us on the subject of mental maladies, their symptoms, and their treatment. But whatever the discoveries of science about the connection between the life of the soul and that of the body, nothing proves that man is not open to the influence of demons. It cannot be affirmed that all mental maladies are of a spiritual nature or origin, but neither can it be affirmed that demoniac influences have no connection with mental maladies; what is called hallucination may be considered—at least sometimes—as a vision of the spiritual world, not in its luminous, but in its dark aspect. Aside from this direct vision, which so many occultists are engaged in investigating, the influence of the powers of darkness is exercised in imperceptible fashion, spiritually. The sacrament of baptism is preceded by "the prayers of the catechumens," which include four prayers where the demoniacal powers are exorcised and summoned to leave the newly baptized.

CHAPTER 9

THE ORTHODOX CHURCH SERVICE

The Orthodox cult, by its beauty and variety, is unique in all Christianity. It unites the heights of Christian inspiration with the most precious heritage of antiquity received from Byzantium. The vision of spiritual beauty is joined to that of the beauty of this world. Russia, so gifted in the arts, has added to that sacred heritage an element of novelty and freshness in such a manner that the Russian Church becomes the continuation of Byzantium. Each of the historic branches of universal Christianity has received a special gift, a characteristic of its own. Catholicism has received the gift of organization and administration, Protestantism the ethical gift of probity of life and of intellectual honesty while on the Orthodox peoples—and especially Byzantium and Russia—has fallen the gift of perceiving the beauty of the spiritual world. And this inner vision, this contemplation, artistic and spiritual, expresses itself outwardly in the forms of piety of the Orthodox cult. This, ''heaven upon earth,'' is the manifestation of the beauty of the spiritual world.[1]

In the Orthodox service, the element of beauty, the glory of God filling the Temple, occupies a place of its own, side by side with prayer and edification; it is, at least in its fundamental tendency, a spiritual art which of itself gives the sense of ''the sweetness of the Church.'' It is natural that, in certain cases, this element should be capable of evoking a too exclusive, exaggerated zeal; the rite then becomes something absolute and fixed. This was the case with the Russian Old Believers of the seventeenth century.

Another trait of the Orthodox service is its religious realism. It is not only the commemoration, in artistic forms, of evangelical or

[1]See my article: ''Le ciel sur la terre,'' in a collection on Oriental Christianity, *Una Sancta*, Munich, 1928. See also *Das Oestliche Christentum. Hesg.* von Prof. K. Ehrenberg. 2 vols. Articles of different authors, particularly my own: ''Die Kosmodicee.''

other events concerning the Church. It is also the actualization of these facts, their reenactment on the earth. During the service of Christmas there is not merely the memory of the birth of Christ, but truly Christ is born in a mysterious manner, just as at Easter He is resurrected. It is the same in the Transfiguration, the Entry into Jerusalem, the mystery of the Last Supper, the Passion, the burial and the Ascension of Christ, and also of all the events of the life of the Holy Virgin, from the Nativity to the Dormition. The life of the Church, in these services, makes actual for us the mystery of the Incarnation. Our Lord continues to live in the Church in the same form in which He was manifested once on earth and which exists for ever, and it is given to the Church to make living these sacred memories so that we should be their new witnesses and participate in them. This is particularly the significance of the Gospel readings which form a part of the liturgy. It may be said in speaking of all Bible readings, but especially in regard to the most important New Testament events—that they are not simply commemorations, but they happen again in the Church.

The whole Office takes on the value of a divine life of which the Temple is the fitting locality. This trait is manifest in the very architecture of the Orthodox Church, whether it is the dome of St. Sophia in Constantinople, which so admirably represents the heaven of Divine Wisdom reflected on earth, or whether it is the cupola of stone or wood of a Russian village church full of sweetness and warmth—the impression is the same. The Gothic temple rises tensely toward the transcendent, but in spite of this unnatural striving toward the heights, there is always the feeling of an unsurmountable distance, yet unattained. Under the Orthodox dome, on the other hand, there is the feeling of life in the house of the Father, after the union between divine and human was realized. Such is the fundamental sentiment of Orthodoxy, which is directly reflected in its cult. The entire Orthodox service is testimony to that conception of life and its realization, to the intimate knowledge of the humanization or incarnation of God, crowned by the Resurrection. Because of this attitude, Orthodoxy truly possesses such knowledge and joy as the first Christians possessed. Certainly it has not the outwards implicity of primitive Christianity, for it carries the burden of the richness and complexity of all the centuries. But beneath this heavy covering of gold there flows the living water, a faith sincere and simple, the knowledge of Christ, the light of the Resurrection.

The mysteries of the Orthodox cult reach their culminating point and their greatest power in the services of Holy Week and Easter. The beauty, the richness and the power of these services take possession of the soul and sweep it along as upon a mystic torrent. Toward the end of the first days of Holy Week, the anointing of the feet of Our Lord by the sinner (Wednesday) leads us to Holy Thursday, to the institution of the Eucharist. Then the rites of Good Friday reproduce in all their power the Passion, the death and burial of Our Lord. During the service of the Passion, with its reading of the twelve passages from the Gospels, followed by appropriate chants, the faithful feel truly near the Cross. Following a pious custom, the lighted candles, held during the Scripture readings, are afterwards taken to their homes. And the picture of all the congregation with their lighted candles, carried through the dark streets, reminds one irresistibly of the light that "shineth in darkness and the darkness received it not." During the vesper service on Good Friday the image of the dead Christ ("The Winding Sheet") is placed in the middle of the church; this is put on an elevated place, as though upon a catafalque, and the faithful venerate it, weeping and embracing it. Those who seek parallels in religious history on the subject of a god, dead and resurrected, discern in this service a resemblance to similar solemnities in the burial of Dionysius, Osiris, Tammuz, etc. But these pagan presentments and these personages only augment the force and the meaning of the Christian rite, which carries in itself—consciously or not—the heritage of antiquity, freed from pagan narrowness.

The office following, the Entombment, constitutes matins of Holy Saturday. This is the culminating point of the Orthodox liturgical creation. The ritual of the burial of Christ is made up of special praises, alternating with verses of Psalm 119. The figure of Old

Testament justice, traced in the psalm, joins admirably with the figure of the New Testament, that of Christ, Who descends to earth and even to hell, but Who nevertheless lives in the heavens. The Winding Sheet is carried three times about the Church to suggest the burial. Afterwards comes the wonderful liturgy of Holy Saturday, during which, after fifteen readings from the Old Testament, the clergy take off their black vestments to put on white. It is then that the first announcement of the Resurrection sounds, at first in sacred hymns, then in the Gospel of the Resurrection. These services of Byzantine origin have found a new fatherland in Russia, which accepted them and reclothed them with its love and beauty. To see the offices of the Passion in Russia, in Moscow or in the country, in the cities or the provinces, is to learn to know the supreme heavenly reality they reveal. Holy Week is the heart of Orthodox rites. It may be said that it is anticipated and prepared for during the whole year. Great are the joy and beauty of the services of the great feasts—as the Annunciation, Christmas, the Epiphany, Pentecost, the Assumption—but all the services pale before the beauty of the grandiose rites of Lent and above all of Holy Week.

And the luminaries themselves pale, as stars of the night before the light of the rising sun, before the light and the joy of the night of Easter. The resurrection of Christ is a high festival in the whole Christian world, but nowhere is it so luminous as in Orthodoxy, and nowhere—I dare add—is it celebrated as in Russia, just at the moment when spring begins with all its sweetness and transparence. The night of Easter, its joy, its exaltation, transport us to the life to come, in new joy, the joy of joys, a joy without end. Before midnight the faithful gather in church to bid farewell to the image of Christ which is carried out before the beginning of matins. At midnight the bells ring and the great door of the sanctuary opens. To the sound of the hymn, ''The angels sing in heaven Thy Resurrection, O Saviour Christ,'' the priests, light in hand, advance in the midst of a perfect sea of candles in the hands of the faithful and before all the icons. To the throbbing of the bells, the procession marches around the outside of the church, then stops before the closed doors of the temple. These latter symbolize the sealed tomb, where the angel comes to roll away the stone. Then the doors of the Church are opened and the priests enter, chanting triumphantly: ''Christ is risen from the dead.'' It is as though a stone had been lifted from the souls of all the worshippers, for they have seen the Resurrection of Christ. Then the matins of Easter begins, matins which consist entirely of the Paschal canon, full of gaiety and of joy divine, and as it pours forth, the priests go to greet the people, to give and receive the kiss of Easter. All embrace each other, saying: ''Christ is risen''—''He is risen indeed.'' It is really the primitive Church, that Christianity of the early times which the wise and the learned seek to understand: ''Come and see.'' The use of the greeting and the Paschal kiss are observed all the week of Easter, not merely in the churches, but in homes and even in the streets.

The feast of Easter is the heart of Orthodoxy, and at the same time a living testimony to its plenitude and truth. It is at once the palpable action of the Holy Spirit, the manifestation of Pentecost, and a manifestion of Christ risen on earth, an invisible manifestion, because it happens after the Ascension. If we wish confirmation of the idea that the church services are not only commemorations but that the event commemorated really happens in the heart of the Orthodox service, we will find it on Easter night, a service which is vitally connected with the Passion as shadows with light, sadness with joy, suffering with happiness. But in the light of eternity, in the light of the Resurrection of Christ, that sadness is extinguished and disappears; it becomes simply a remembrance of something past. A Paschal hymn expresses this sentiment: ''Yesterday I was buried with Thee, O Christ; with Thee to-day I rise from the dead.''

As in all Christianity, the Eucharistic liturgy forms the center of the Orthodox office. This liturgy is celebrated according to the an cient rites of St. Basil the Great and of St. John Chrysostom. The ''liturgy of the Presanctified Gifts'' by St. Gregory, Pope of Rome, is also used. Compared with the more recent Western mass, the Orthodox liturgy is longer, Together with the parts common to both (the reading of the Epistle and Gospel, the "Eucharistic canon"), it includes certain elements lacking in the Catholic mass, notably the preparation of the holy gifts, during which memorials are made of the Saints, the dead and the living, and where portions of the altar bread are disposed according to their intention. During the Eucharist not only are the holy gifts consecrated, but by symbolic acts, readings and prayers, the whole mystery of the incarnation is renewed from the Grotto of Bethlehem to the Mount of Olives, from the Nativity to the Ascension. The consecration of the holy gifts attributed by Western theology to the moment when the priest pronounces the words of Christ, "this is My Body" . . . "this is my Blood," this consecration is effected—according to Orthodox thought—during the whole liturgy, beginning with the "preparation." It is completed at the moment when the words of Our Lord are pronounced and when the Holy Spirit is invoked ("epiclesis"). Both laity and clergy communicate under both species, the Body and Blood of Christ. Orthodoxy has preserved that ancient usage, which Catholicism has lost in spite of the words of the Lord: "Drink ye all of this." The faithful present at the liturgy without receiving communion participate in spirit in the Eucharistic repast and eat the blessed bread from which the eucharistic elements were taken before their consecration. For Communion of the sick and dying in their homes, the holy gifts are preserved in a casket on the altar, but they are never exposed for adoration outside the liturgy, as in Catholicism.

In addition to the liturgy there are many daily Orthodox services such as matins, "the hours," vespers, compline, vigil, and forms for feasts and other special occasions. The Orthodox Office is an extremely complex unit, composed of fixed parts (fixed readings, prayers and chants), and changeable parts (such as those for festivals of the Saints and sometimes a union of several services). The rules of the Orthodox Office are determined by special law, the "typicon," which is an amalgam of the ritual of the Monastery of St. Sava of Jerusalem and that of St. Theodore the Studite of Byzantium. Nevertheless, the strict observance of these monastic rituals would be too difficult, and they are simplified in order to adapt them to the needs of our day. The Office reflects the whole history of the Church; it is an historical conglomorate. The very character of many hymns of the Church show their Byzantine origin; they are pompous and sometimes difficult to understand. But the services of great feasts offer us unique examples of poetic and religious inspiration. Their translation into Old Slavonic, by its artistic character, is entirely worthy of the original.

The Orthodox Office is composed above all of readings from the Old Testament, the psalms—a permanent part of practically all services, readings from the Pentateuch, the prophetic and historical books and from all the books of the New Testament (the Apocalypse excepted), according to an established order. Afterwards come the litanies, or special prayers of supplication, other prayers, and finally sacred chants of different types (canons, "stichiri"). Their content is historical, edifying, prayerful. In addition there are fixed homilies, read especially in monasteries. Preaching is also part of the Office, but it does not have the exclusive importance given it by Protestantism, because the Office itself is full of elements of edification. It is so instructive of itself, that special preaching is not always necessary. In spite of this, preaching occupies an important place in the Orthodox service, and a sermon by the priest or bishop, during the liturgy, after the reading of the Gospel or at the end of the service is the usual custom.

The Orthodox service does not involve such extensive participation by the whole congregation as is the case in Protestantism. Reading and singing are done by specially appointed persons, the readers and the choir, and it is only rarely that the whole congregation participates in the singing. On the other hand, Orthodoxy does not use musical instruments during the offices. There is no organ, no orchestra which, as substitute for the human voice, for the word, for the praises chanted by man, mechanical sounds without words, without meaning although musically beautiful, tends to make the service "worldly." This would not fit the sober spirit of Orthodoxy, which is not reconciled to replacing spiritual elevation by esthetic emotion. On the contrary, the beauty of the human voice, especially in choral chants, is much appreciated in the Orthodox Church. Russian church choirs are celebrated everywhere, but the full value of the beauty of Old Church motifs is still insufficiently known and appreciated, preserved as it is in what is called "usage" in the traditional cycle of Orthodox Church music.

Besides common offices and personal prayers, obligatory for all the faithful, there are particular services, appropriate to the special needs of this or that person. First comes the administration of the Holy Mysteries, then the prayers and the rites demanded by individual needs. Services of special intercession are widespread: prayers for the sick, for travellers, for prisoners, for scholars, services of special thanksgiving, as well as prayers specially addressed to a Saint for a certain person. The prayers for the dead and funeral services are of great importance. The Orthodox Church always remembers the dead, both during the liturgy (above all the liturgy for the repose of the souls), and during special services among which such prayers have the most prominent place. The Church prays for the repose of the soul and the remission of the sins of the dead. It believes in the efficacy of these prayers, above all of the eucharistic sacrifice, to lighten the destinies beyond the tomb. The Orthodox Church has no doctrine of Purgatory as a special place or state in which the dead must suffer their punishment, but it believes that our prayers for the dead can aid them, and even snatch from hell and lead to paradise those whose condition does not present unsurmountable obstacles. The ritual of funeral services is particularly touching and beautiful, producing an irresistible impression, even on persons belonging to other confessions.

One trait of the Orthodox Office must be noted particularly—that is its cosmic quality. It is addressed not only to the human soul but to all creation, and it sanctifies the latter. This sanctification of the elements of nature and of different objects expresses the idea that the sanctifying action of the Holy Spirit is extended by the Church over all nature. The destiny of nature is allied to that of man; corrupted because of man, she awaits with him her healing. On the other hand, Our Lord, having taken on Himself true humanity, has joined His life to all of nature. He walked on this earth, He looked at its flowers and its plants, its birds, its fish, its animals, He ate of its fruits. He was baptized in the water of Jordan, He walked on its waters, He rested in the womb of the earth, and there is nothing in all creation (outside of evil and sin) which remains foreign to His humanity. So the Church blesses all creation; it blesses the flowers, the plants, the branches brought to the Church for the Feast of the Holy Trinity, the fruits brought for that of the Transfiguration; certain foods are blessed during the night of Easter, different places and objects according to particular needs. Among these special services we must note the solemn consecration of a church by which it becomes a place worthy of the service of the Office and of the divine Eucharist, as well as the offices for the sanctification of different objects of the cult, vestments, vessels, bells, etc. The Church also blesses the Chrism for the sacrament of Chrismation and oil for many needs, the Eucharistic bread (''prosphora'') and the extraliturgical bread, the wine, etc. The benediction of waters happens on the eve of the Feast of the Epiphany and on the day of that feast. It can be performed, however, at any time at the request of anyone, and the water may be drunk or used to sprinkle holy objects and places. This rite sanctifies the aquatic element in general.

The meaning and the foundation of all these rites is that they both precede and prepare the new creature, the transfiguration of all creation, ''the new earth and the new heaven.'' Rationalism easily discovers ''magic'' here, or pagan superstition, because it seems to confine the force of Christianity to the limits of the spiritual world of man. But man is a spirit incarnated, a cosmic being; the cosmos lives in him, it is sanctified in him, for the Lord is not only Saviour of souls, but of bodies, also, and consequently of the entire world. Hence the cosmic quality of the Orthodox office expresses that fullness of Christianity, and the Lord who sanctified the earth and the waters of the Jordan continues to bless them by His Spirit present in the Church. From this it is clear that the sanctification of nature is allied to the sanctification of the spirit. We become sanctified ourselves when we eat a holy substance. In the Eucharist the matter of the world is sanctified by becoming the Body and Blood of Christ, and it is given to us to be in communion with Him. But the elements used in the Eucharist form part of the whole world of matter, and its sanctification by what may well be called a renewed Incarnation of God implies all previous blessings which are but inferior degrees of the same.

Among the objects blessed by the cult we should mention first the material of the cult itself, the various sacred objects, especially vessels and priestly vestments. The latter date from most ancient times: thanks to their Byzantine origin they preserve the traits of classic antiquity. The meaning of these vestments is that man cannot approach a holy place in his accustomed state. He must change and put on holy vestments which form a sort of impenetrable cover about him. The use of incense, of lighted candles, of silver and gold as ornaments of the temple, of vestments, of icons, etc.—all this is directly connected with the mystic side of the Office, with the sense of the real presence of God in the Church.

The grandeur and the beauty of the mystery of the Orthodox service act on the intelligence, the feeling and the imagination of all those present at it. An old legend says that our ancestors, the Russians who sought the true faith, and who were present at a service in St. Sophia in Constantinople, declared they knew not where they were on earth or in heaven. This method of coming to know the heart of Orthodoxy is, of course, very difficult for a Western Christian, but it is the most intimate and the surest, for the heart of Orthodoxy is found in its rites.

CHAPTER 10

ICONS AND THEIR CULT

The veneration of holy icons occupies an important place in Orthodox piety. The icons represent Our Lord Jesus Christ, the Holy Virgin, the angels and the Saints, but the Cross and the Gospel receive the same veneration. Orthodox churches are covered, in the interior, with mural decorations and much ornamented with icons, placed on the iconostasis (the partition which separates the sanctuary from the nave) and on the walls. These pictures are usually painted on wooden panels or any other plain surface. Statues and sculpture in general, in contrast to the custom in Western churches, are rare in Orthodox temples. From the canonical point of view, the cult of icons is based on the definition of the seventh ecumenical council, which has the force of law for the Church. It has its basis, as well, in religious psychology, a basis so profound that the icon seems indispensable to Orthodox piety. In the "golden ages" of Orthodoxy—in both Byzantium and Russia—icons filled the churches; they were put everywhere, in the houses, in the streets, in the squares, in public buildings. A dwelling without icons often affects an Orthodox as empty. In travelling, when he visits strange places, the Orthodox sometimes carries an icon, before which he says his prayers. He also wears on his neck the little cross which he received at baptism. The icon gives the real feeling of the presence of God.

The use of icons is very rarely understood in the West, even in Catholicism, in spite of the fact that the latter recognizes the propriety of such veneration. In Protestantism, which perpetuates the tradition of the iconoclasts, and where icons are limited to the picture of Christ, the veneration of icons is often held to be idolatry. This is because of a refusal to study the problem and to discover the true meaning of icons. The use of icons is based on the belief that God can be represented in man, who, since the creation, possesses the image of God (Gen. 1:26), although obscured by original sin. God cannot be represented in His eternal being, but, in His revelation to man, He has an appearance, He can be described. Otherwise, the revelation of God could not take place.[1] The events of the earthly life of Our Lord Jesus Christ are specially subject to representation in pictures. They are pictured in words in the Holy Gospel, which, in this sense, is a verbal icon of Christ. Religious pictures, representing evangelical events, meet with no objection in principle, even among Protestants. They are used for the purpose of teaching, of reminders of events in sacred history, or of inspiration. Used thus, just as are sacred texts, for the beautification of the temple, they are also nothing other than for the edification of the worshippers. This purpose is served in Orthodoxy by the mural paintings which cover its church walls but do not serve the purpose of true icons. The icon is not only a holy picture, it is something greater than a mere picture. According to Orthodox belief, an icon is a place of the Gracious Presence. It is the place of an appearance of Christ, of the Virgin, of the Saints, of all those represented by the icon, and hence it serves as a place for prayer to them.

This semblance of Christ before which the prayers of the faithful are said, His image, made only of wood and color, materials necessary for that representation, does not belong to the Body of Christ. In this sense the icon is the opposite of the Eucharist, where there is no image of Christ, but where He is mysteriously present in matter in His Body and Blood, offered to the communicant. The Orthodox prays before the icon of Christ as before Christ Himself; but the icon, the abiding place of that presence, remains only a thing and never becomes an idol or a fetish. The need to have before one an icon is evidence of the concrete character of a religious sentiment which often cannot be satisfied by contemplation alone, and which seeks an immediate approach to the divine. This is natural, for man consists of both a spirit and a body. The veneration of holy icons is based not merely on the nature of the subjects represented

[1]For the dogmatic basis of the cult of icons, see my book *The Icon and the Veneration of Icons* (in Russian), 1930.

in them, but also on the faith in that gracious presence which the Church calls forth by the power of sanctification of the icon.

The rite of the blessing of the icon establishes a connection between the image and its prototype, between that which is represented and the representation itself. By the blessing of the icon of Christ, a mystical meeting of the faithful and Christ is made possible. It is the same with the icons of the Virgin and the Saints; their icons, one may say, prolong their lives here below. The veneration of holy relics has a similar significance. By the power of this gracious presence, aid may be given the worshipper, in a sense as though it came from the person represented in the icon, and in this sense every icon which has received its full power, by the fact of having been blessed, is in principle a wonder-working icon. As a matter of fact, only those icons are considered wonder-working which have revealed themselves as possessing miraculous power, expressing this power in some specially evident way.

Wonder-working icons of the Mother of God are specially numerous. The Church believes that the Holy Virgin, who in the person of the Apostle John adopted the whole human race, the whole Church, did not leave the world at the time of her Dormition. Although she remains in heaven, she still lives with us the life of our world, suffers with its suffering, and weeps with its tears. She intercedes for the world before the throne of God. She reveals herself to the world in her wonder-working icons, which represent the traces of her existence on earth. This Orthodox belief is shared by Catholicism as well.

The object of icons is the representation of Christ, of the Holy Trinity (particularly in the form of the three angels of the vision of Abraham, near the oak of Mamre), of the Holy Virgin, the angels and the Saints. The subject of these icons is not limited to a single figure, but many include entire incidents in the life of Christ (icons of feasts) and can express very complicated dogmatic matters (different icons of St. Sophia, the Holy Wisdom, "cosmic" icons of the Virgin, etc.). What is the origin of such icons? It is determined in part by the direct principles of the Word of God, in part by theological considerations (in this sense these icons are scholastic paintings); in addition icons may represent spiritual visions accorded to a certain man. (In Western iconography the works of Fra Angelico in particular have this character of visions.) As such, these visions, received by the Church by means of the icon, become a new revelation, a source of thelogical ideas (this is the case in the problem of the Divine Wisdom) from which an iconographic theology is born. In general, the icon is an aspect of ecclesiastical tradition in colors and images, parallel to oral, written and monumental tradition. The making of icons (which in mass production tends to become a mere trade) is, in its original purity, a work of religious creation. The Church has glorified certain Saints specially as painters of icons. The two greatest masters of Russian iconography may be cited as examples, the two friends, the Venerable Andrey Rublev and Dionysius, both monks. It is only very rarely, however, that the names of icon painters are known. Like the Gothic cathedrals of the West, icons usually remain anonymous. Certainly true visions of the divine, theological contemplation expressed by an image occur only seldom, but these exceptions become models for copying in the production of the mass of icons in ordinary use.

The icon, then, is religious contemplation reclothed in images, colors and forms. It is a revelation under artistic form; it is not abstract idea, but concrete form. This is why the symbolism of colors, the rhythm of lines, the spacing of the composition are so important in iconography. The visions of the spiritual world are reclothed in artistic form where the language of colors (gold, silver, azure, blue, green, purple, etc.) and the lines receive an exceptional value in the exceedingly limited scale of artistic means. In principle, everything in the icon is symbolic, everything has a meaning; not only the subject, but the forms and colors also. To know and to preserve the symbolic meaning of the icon—this is the tradition of iconographic painting, which dates from most ancient times, perhaps even from pre-Christian antiquity, Greek or Egyptian, and which was inherited by Christian Byzantium. Thus there is formed an iconographic "canon," preserved in all its purity in the oldest icons. The Russian "Old Believers" who have lovingly preserved these old icons have done special service here. They are equalled in value by modern science, which has revealed these icons to the world, as chefs-d'oeuvre worthy to be compared with the world's greatest productions.

As we have said, there exists a certain canon for the painting of each icon, the "original" which indicates how a given Saint or event should be represented. This canon dates from the earliest times. To be sure, it has only a general, directive value. It not only leaves room for personal inspiration and for the creative spirit (which insensibly modifies it), but even presupposes such creativeness. There is no such thing, therefore, as an absolute canon of the icon, as the Old Believers think. Such a canon would condemn the painting of icons to complete immobility and to death in so far as art is concerned. Icons are born of art and should remain in the realm of art. While founded on tradition and developing it, the icon has its own life and its place in modern art. The art of the icon has a great and wonderful future. Meanwhile that art is not the slave of the canon as an exterior law, but freely accepts it as a vision of ancient and interior truth. The painting of icons is a branch of symbolic art, but more than that, it is a vision of God, a knowledge of God, a testimony given in the realm of art.

Truly to attain to this art of the icon, an artist and a contemplative theologian must be united in the same person. Art alone cannot create an icon, nor can theology alone. This is why the real painting of icons is the rarest and most difficult of the arts. It demands the combination of these two gifts, each rare in itself. Nevertheless, the results and the revelations of icon painting surpass, in power, both speculative theology and profane art. Icon painting testifies to the beyond and its aspects; it does not attempt to prove, it simply presents. It does not constrain by the power of proofs; it convinces and conquers by its very evidence.

In its purpose of revealing the mysteries of the spiritual world, iconography has its special characteristics. First of all it is foreign to that naturalism or realism which gained the ascendancy in the Renaissance. The painting of icons does not permit sensuality in its pictures; they must remain formal, abstract, schematic, they consist only in form and color. Such painting seeks to portray the image of the Saint rather than the face. It is a stranger to impressionism, but in its distinct forms, its precise colors, it approaches decorative art. Hence, icons do not know a third dimension; they have no depth, but content themselves, like Egyptian painting, with flat representation and reverse perspective, which excludes sensuality and leads to the predominance of forms and colors with their symbolism. This is why the artistic methods of icon painting have a severe and ascetic character, and cannot have sensuality, carnal voluptuousness. The painting of the pictures is severe, serious; it may even appear dry, as all elevated and pure art will always seem, to the children of the flesh.

The artistic homeland of the icon is ancient Egypt (particularly the funerary portraits of the Hellenistic epoch). Byzantium, inheritor and continuer of ancient Greece, is the homeland of Christian iconography. Here such painting passed through several periods of flowering. From Byzantium the art of the icon was carried to the Balkan countries and to Russia, where it attained the highest degree of development in the fifteenth century at Moscow and Novgorod. The problem of the connection between Italian painting and the art of the Russian icon is still the subject of scientific discussion.

The influence of the West is clearly felt in icon painting when its decadence begins, about the sixteenth century. Simon Ushakov (Moscow, seventeenth century) is a representative of this tendency, although not without talent. In the eighteenth centuries the influence of Western taste on Russian art lowered the standards of the latter. Traits of naturalism and of dilettantism appeared; the characteristic Russian style was wiped out, and the art of the icon became a profession. It is only in these latter days that the comprehension of icon painting as an art has begun anew. At the same time there is reborn a knowledge of the true and elevated aims of that art, which promises a new period of flowering.

CHAPTER 11

ORTHODOX MYSTICISM

"Mysticism" is an interior experience which leads to the attainment of the spiritual, divine world. It may also be an interior perception (and not only interior) of the natural world. For mysticism to be possible, man must have a special capacity for immediate and superrational and supersensual conception, the capacity for intuitive perception which we rightly call "mystic." We must distinguish between this and the state of mind which borders on the subjective-psychological condition. Mystic experience has an objective character; it is founded on a departure from one's own narrow limitations and a resultant spiritual contact or encounter. Saul, on the road to Damascus, was not the victim of an illusion or an hallucination, which had only a subjective meaning: Saul saw a real vision of Christ, which, nevertheless, remained invisible to the companions of Saul, who heard only the voice. In reality, that vision was revealed to his interior feeling; it was mystic. All the life of Orthodoxy is full of heavenly visions. This is what is essential in Orthodoxy, something which its travelling companions do not see, and thus they do not see its inner meaning, but only what seem to them its external "petrified" or "mummified" forms.

The whole life of Orthodoxy is bound up with visions of the other world. Without that vision Orthodoxy would not exist.[1] The divine office comprehends, as I have indicated above, not only the commemoration, but the reality of great events. The faithful, in proportion to their spiritual development, share in the life of Our Lord, of the Virgin and the Saints, and in that way communicate with the world invisible. This mystic realism serves as the foundation for all the Orthodox services; without it, the Office would lose all its power, power to be the eternal actualization of the mystery of the

---

[1] See my essay: "Le ciel sur la terre," *Una Sancata*, 1928, IV.

145

Incarnation. Hence the Orthodox Office is directed first of all to the mystic sentiment, to arouse and minister to it.

Among all the sacraments and sacramentals, the Holy Eucharist, center of Orthodox piety, has an essential fundamental value. The Communion of the Body and Blood of Christ have always been the principal source of the prayer, of the meditation, and above all of the Eucharistic vision of Christ. Like the summit of a mountain, the Eucharist seems greater in proportion as one approaches it, whether exteriorly or interiorly. Holy Communion has always had a special importance in the life of the Saints, as their biographies testify.

Holy Communion is a reliving of the miracle of the Incarnation. It is a constant presentation of man before the face of God. It gives man a meeting-place with Christ, fills all his being with mystic and exalted emotion. Man enters into contact with a higher world, and it enters into his life.

The Orthodox mystery of Holy Communion is free from sensuality; it is rather distinguished by its sobriety. The adoration of the Holy Gifts, apart from the Communion itself, is unknown in Orthodoxy. Equally unknown are the cult of the heart of Jesus, the heart of the Virgin, the "five wounds," etc. In general, Orthodox spirituality does not encourage that type of imagination which enables man to represent spiritual things to himself and to relive them by means of the senses. The imagery contained in the prayers of the Church and the icons, with those of the Gospel, are sufficient to enable man to enter in spirit into the events commemorated. All man's imagination is sullied by his subjectivity and, what is worse, his sensuality; that is of little use in the truly mystical life.

Orthodox mysticism is without imagery; without imagery, also, is the way which leads to it, that is, prayer and meditation. These should not result in God's being represented by human means, unless God Himself gives these images to man. In conformity with this characteristic of Orthodox mysticism, a most important means to the life of prayer is the name of God, invoked in prayer. The ascetics and all those who lead a life of prayer, from the anchorites of the Thebaid and the "hesychasts" of Mt. Athos to Fr. John of

Kronstadt, insist above all on the importance of the Name of God. Aside from the offices, there is a "rule of prayer," valid for all Orthodox, composed of psalms and different petitions; for monks it is much greater than for laymen.

But what is most important in the work of prayer, that which constitutes its very heart, is what is called the prayer of Jesus: "Lord Jesus Christ, Son of God, have mercy on me a sinner." This prayer, repeated hundreds of times and even indefinitely, forms the essential element of the whole monastic rule. It may, if need be, replace the Office and all other prayers, such is its universal value. The power of this prayer is not in its content, which is simple and clear (it is the prayer of the publican), but in the "most sweet name of Jesus." The ascetics testify that this Name has in itself the power of the presence of God. Not only is God invoked by this Name, but He is already present in the invocation. This may be said, of course, of every name of God, but it is especially true of the divine and human name of Jesus, a name belonging to both God and man. In short, the name of Jesus, present in the human heart, gives it the power of deification which Our Redeemer accorded us.

The prayer of Jesus, according to the testimony of the ascetics, has three degrees or aspects. At first it is oral prayer; an effort is made to have constantly on the lips and in spirit the prayer of Jesus (on condition, of course, that the state of the soul is suitably attuned and the believer is living in peace and love with all, observing the commandments, being chaste and humble). It is still very difficult, at this stage, to say the prayer of Jesus for a long time and, so far as possible, continuously. It is a painful work, an effort which seems to be unrewarded. In the second state, the prayer of Jesus becomes mental or psychic. The mind begins to enter into that prayer, constantly repeated, and concentrates on the name of Jesus; already the power of Christ, hidden in it, is revealed. Then the mind, freed from its errors, continues and rests in "the hidden chamber" of meditation on God. Here already there is a foretaste of the sweetness of the name of Jesus. Finally the third supreme degree of "spiritual action" (this is the name applied to the prayer of Jesus) is reached in the spirit or in the heart. At this stage the prayer of Jesus is said as of itself in the heart, constantly and without any effort and, shining through the heart, the light of the name of Jesus illuminates all the universe. This state cannot be described in words, but is already the prototype of that where ''God shall be all in all.'' This distinction between the three degrees is, of course, only a plan, a sketch of the interior way of the prayer of Jesus which constitutes the essential type of Orthodox mysticism.

The practical application of the prayer of Jesus has naturally led to theological discussion on the name of God and its power, on the meaning of the veneration of the name of God and on its active force. These questions have not yet received solutions having the value of dogma for a whole Church. They have not, on the other hand, been sufficiently considered by theological literature. For the moment two different tendencies exist: one group (who designate themselves as ''glorifiers of the name of God'') are partisans of realism in the understanding of the meaning of the name in general. They believe that the name of God, invoked in prayer, immediately contains the presence of God (Fr. John of Kronstadt and others). Others hold a more rationalistic and nominalistic view, according to which the name of God is a human, instrumental means for the expression of human striving towards God. Those who practise the Jesus prayer and the mystics in general, as well as certain theologians and hierarchs, are partisans of the first opinion. The second point of view is characteristic of the school of Orthodox theology which has reflected European rationalism. In any case, the theological doctrine of the name of God is a problem of the present time, a problem essential to the expression and comprehension of Orthodoxy, a problem which our epoch bequeaths to the future. This problem is one of the principal indications along the way of contemporary Orthodox theological thought. The same is true of the problem of the Divine Wisdom or Sophia, which we shall not consider here because of its complexity.

In Orthodoxy there are many mystical works, of great practical religious value, devoted to prayer in general and in particular to the "prayer of Jesus." We should first note the great collection called "Philokalia" (5 vols.) and an entire series of ascetic works, those of Ephraim the Syrian, Isaac the Syrian, John Climacus and the modern spiritual authors: Bishop Theophan the Recluse, Bishop Ignatius Brianchaninov, the Holy Bishop Tikhon, Fr. John of Kronstadt, and others.

The value of prayer consists, first, in its orienting the spirit towards God; it is a conversation with God. But the principal power of prayer, as of the Christian life, is to lead the Christian to the acquisition of the Holy Spirit. Those who live in Christ bear within themselves the Holy Spirit, and inversely, those who have the Spirit learn the meaning of the words "It is not I who live, it is Christ Who liveth in me." This "Spirit-bearing" baffles exact description, but it is instantly felt when one comes into the presence of such a person, as an "other" spiritual life within the human life. It is just this seal of the Spirit of God, this bearing of the Spirit, which the Orthodox soul seeks and desires above all and which it venerates most. This bearing of the Spirit, which corresponds to the ministry of the prophets of the Old Testament, is in Christianity connected with the prophetic ministry of Christ Who was anointed by the Holy Spirit. The "elders," the "spirituals" (pneumatophores) in Orthodoxy, all those infused by the Spirit, are in this sense Christian prophets or prophetesses (for this ministry does not, like the priestly office, belong only to the masculine sex). The bearing of the Spirit is in no way allied to the hieratic dignity, but may, as a matter of fact, be found in conjunction with it. The great figures of the Saints, as for example St. Sergius or St. Seraphim, give us an idea of what the prophets of Christianity may be, and the disciples who surround them give us an idea of the prophetic schools.

St. Seraphim of Sarov (end of the seventeenth, beginning of the eighteenth century) is a striking type of "pneumatophore" in the Russian Church. His disciple Motovilov relates that St. Seraphim revealed to him the Holy Spirit resident in him. St. Seraphim, said Motovilov, began to shine like the sun in flashing radiance. This event happened in winter in the midst of snow, and nevertheless

Motovilov felt a fragrant warmth and a celestial joy. When the phenomenon ceased, St. Seraphim appeared before him in his accustomed aspect. Almost of our time, the ''elders'' of the monastery of Optina (Fr. Ambrose and others) showed themselves to be sublime examples of the ''Spirit-bearers.'' From all corners of Russia pilgrims came by thousands to these elders. Fr. John of Kronstadt was equally well known.

The image of Christ shines in the Christian soul, and shows it the way of life. Christianity cannot have another way of life, another ideal, than to become like Christ Himself (Gal. 4:19). But the image of Christ is universal, and every soul seeks in Christ its own image; from this flows a diversity of spiritual gifts. In this sense, that the Christian way is one's own, it may be said that each man and each people has its own Christ. The Catholic world loves above all the humanity of Christ, the Christ as suffering, crucified. To be crucified with Him, to live with Him, His Passion and the Cross, this is perhaps what is essential in Catholic mysticism; characterized by the stigmata, the way of the Cross, the cult of the five wounds, etc. Certainly for all Christianity, the Passion of Christ is sacred; the whole Christian world bows before the Cross. In Orthodoxy on Holy Thursday, the reading of the ''Twelve Gospels'' of the Passion is one of the high points of the liturgical year; the Church weeps in silence, embracing in spirit the wounds of Christ. And each week, on Wednesday and Friday, there are offices devoted to the Cross. But it is not the image of Christ crucified which has entered into and possessed the soul of the Orthodox people. It is more the image of Christ, meek and lowly, Lamb of God, Who has taken on Himself the sins of the world, and Who has humbled Himself to take a human form; He Who came into this world to serve all men and not to be served; He Who submitted without a murmur to outrage and dishonor, and Who answered these with love.

The way of spiritual poverty, which contains all the other ''beatitudes,'' is, above all, revealed to the Orthodox soul. The sanctity it seeks (the Russian people expressed this tendency by the name ''Holy Russia'') appears in the form of abnegation and

and supreme humility. This is why the "people of God" (the poor and simple) are so characteristic of Orthodoxy, above all Russian Orthodoxy: those who are not of this world and who have here "no abiding city"; pilgrims, the homeless "fools for Christ" who have renounced human reason, accepted the appearance of folly, voluntarily to experience outrages and humiliations for the love of Christ. Certainly Orthodox sanctity is not limited to these forms. But such traits manifest what is most intimate and at the same time heroic in it; all the power of religious will is used to shed the natural form and to put on the Christ. These "people of God," the outwardly powerless, are without defence, as is the whole Russian Church, faced with its persecutors today. Christ, during His Passion, after Gethsemane, did no more miracles, and this human defencelessness, which excluded neither His divine power nor the legions of angels of the Father, is marked with the seal of sublime grandeur; as though Our Lord had shown us how to realize the beatitudes, summoning all who are weary and heavy laden to just this realization. This aspect of holiness, not of this world, must doubtless be completed by work for the love of Christ, but in this world. Nevertheless every aspect of holiness should possess a character not of this world—this is its intimate tendency, the salt, without which all would become worldly; "for the Gentiles seek all these things" (Matt. 6:32), the Gentiles who know not, who do not carry in their hearts the image of the suffering Christ, meek and lowly.

It cannot be denied that Orthodoxy, not as the ecumenical Church, but as Eastern Christianity, wears an aspect which is less "of this world" than that of the Christianity of the West. The West is more practical, the East more contemplative. Eastern Christianity considers as its first apostle the Beloved Disciple whom Christ from the Cross gave as son to His Mother, the Apostle of love. Western Christianity is especially filled with the spirit of the two princes of the Apostles: Peter (Catholicism) and Paul (Protestantism). John wished to rest on the Master's breast, while Peter asked if two swords were enough and concerned himself with the organization of the Church. This explains the contemplative character of monastic life in the East. Here monasticism does not show the variety and the shades of difference evident in Catholic religious orders. Contemplation in the West is proper only to certain orders; in the East it is the characteristic trait of all monastic life. The monastic state in Orthodoxy is ''the acceptance of the angelic form,'' that is the abandonment of the world for the service of prayer and ascetic practices, rather than for fighting in the world ''ad majorem Dei gloriam.'' Certainly the work of Mary and of Martha, the two sisters equally loved by Our Lord, cannot be wholly separated, and still less can they be opposed, but there nevertheless remains a well-marked difference. It is quite possible that Orthodoxy may now turn towards the world, more than it has ever done up to the present; the history of the Church seems to promise it. But it will still retain its spiritual type.

Orthodoxy has the vision of ideal spiritual beauty, to which the soul seeks ways of approach. Greek antiquity knew something of the same kind in its ideal, of the good and the beautiful united. It is the celestial kingdom of ideas which Plato once contemplated; these are images of the angelic world, the spiritual sky which is reflected in earthly waters (Gen. 1:1). It is a religious idea, more esthetic than ethical, an ideal which lies beyond good and evil. It is the light which brightens the way of pilgrims on this earth. This ideal calls us beyond the limits of our present life, it calls us to its transfiguration.

CHAPTER 12

ORTHODOX ETHIC

Orthodoxy knows no such thing as "autonomous ethic" which forms the special spiritual gift of Protestantism. For Orthodoxy, ethic is religious, it is the image of the salvation of the soul. The religious-ethical maximum is attained in the monastic idea: the perfect imitation of Christ in carrying His Cross and in abnegation. The supreme virtues of the monks are humility and purity of heart, attained by renunciation of the will. The vows of poverty and chastity are only means of arriving at this end, although these means are not obligatory for all, as is the end itself. Orthodoxy knows no different standards of morals; it applies the same standard to all the situations of life. Neither does it recognize any distinction between two moralities, one secular and the other monastic; these are only differences of quantity, of degree, and not of nature.

It may seem that the maximalist inflexibility of the monastic ideal makes Orthodox morality other-worldly and separates it from practical existence, so that it has no answer to give to the many different questions of our modern life. It cannot be denied that maximalism is always more difficult than minimalism; the failures and the distortions of maximalism often lead to the worst consequences. But the truth itself is maximalist, it lacks suppleness; while it does not always exist in its fullness, it never compounds with half-truths. The narrow way is the Christian way and it cannot be widened. This is why essential ethical principles suffer no adaptation, no compromise, no concession. Nevertheless, the reproach of "renouncing the world," addressed to Orthodoxy, lacks foundation. It can be applied only to one historical aspect of Orthodoxy, too much influenced by Eastern monasticism and marked by a certain dualist and pseudo-eschatological pessimism. But it can by no means be applied to Orthodoxy as a whole, illuminated by the light of the Trans-

153

figuration and the Resurrection.

From the ethical point of view, Orthodoxy may be defined as health and equilibrium of soul; in spite of its tragic seriousness, proper to a "kingdom not of this world," there is room in it for an optimistic mentality, full of the joy of life within the limits of earthly existence. The monastic state is by no means its only way (and in any case, not always its most difficult way) for the attainment of the precepts of Christ. This becomes evident when the lives of the Saints glorified by the Church are studied. Side by side with heroes of monastic asceticism we find day-laborers, pious soldiers, kings and princes, mothers and wives; here is direct testimony to the almost equal value of divers ways. Each one should be monk and ascetic in his heart. And if it must be said that the monastic ideal is necessary for every Christian, that applies only to interior renunciation for the love of itself. This renunciation makes impossible the excessive attachment to this world, which was the way of paganism. The necessity to resist the world ascetically is so ordered that those who possess should be, according to the words of St. Paul, as those who possess not.

No domain of life is condemned or abolished: "Every one should remain in the state in which he is called" (I Cor. 7:20). But in whatever state one must be Christian. By means of this interior spiritual action, a whole world of Christian "values" is spread abroad in the state, in economics, in civilization; thus is formed what is called the spirit of an epoch. Orthodoxy has shown its power in educating the peoples of the East—Byzantium, Russia, the Slavs; its power has certainly not been exhausted by this effort, and new problems open before it. All the above reveals an historic relativity of means and methods of Orthodox morality, while the end remains one and absolute: likeness to Christ.

We find an especial difficulty, for Orthodox ethic, in a trait already indicated; the ideal foundation of Orthodoxy is not ethic, but religious, esthetic; it is the vision of "spiritual beauty." To gain it one must have a "spiritual art," a creative inspiration. This art remains the privilege of a small number; the others content themselves with the morality which, by itself, has no "spiritual taste"—it does not inspire, it only disciplines. Neither morality of which we see an apotheosis in the rigid and autonomous ethic of Kant, nor the practical "probabilism" in vogue in Catholicism, belong really to Orthodoxy. It cannot be denied that this spiritual estheticism of Orthodoxy sometimes degenerates into indifference concerning practical necessities and above all the methodical training of the will. This has unfortunately been evident in moments of historical crisis. Humility and love are the supreme characteristics of the Orthodox. From these qualities come the modesty, the sincerity, the simplicity which are so incompatible with the spirit of proselytizing, the authoritarian spirit ("compelle intrare") which prevails elsewhere. Orthodoxy does not persuade or try to compel; it charms and attracts; such is its method of working in the world.

Orthodoxy educates the heart; this is its characteristic trait, the source of its superiority and also of its weakness: its lack of education of the will. The Christian ethics developed by the different confessions certainly reflect the differences existing between them. They are affected by the character of the different peoples and bear the mark of their historic destinies. Practical morality, and philanthropy form the domain where the division in the Christian world is least felt.[1]. And I think that, united in this, different Christian peoples, belonging to different confessions, may learn much from each other. The West may find a complement to its dryness in the free spirit of Orthodoxy; the Orthodox East can learn from the Christian West many things in regard to the religious organization of everyday life. For Martha and Mary, while different in many ways, were equally loved by Our Lord.

[1]The Stockholm Movement, *Life and Work*.

CHAPTER 13

ORTHODOXY AND THE STATE

The relationships between Church and state have greatly varied in different epochs. In the eyes of the primitive Church, the pagan state was "the beast wearing the crown adorned with cursings." The Church's feeling toward the state was hostile, eschatological, "for the figure of this world passes," and soon everything would be finished. The transition from eschatology to history is already marked in the Epistles of St. Paul, especially in thirteenth chapter of the Epistle to the Romans, where, face to face with the power of Nero, the Apostle proclaimed the principle: "There is no power but of God," and where he admits the positive value of the state in connection with the historic ways of the Kingdom of God. This is in keeping with all the prophecies, in both Old and New Testament, that the way of the Kingdom of God includes the fate of the pagan world, includes the natural forces active in history, and among these the state.

Thus the relationships between Church and state remained wholly exterior so long as the Roman state remained pagan. But when this state, in the person of the Emperor Constantine, bowed before the Cross, the situation changed. The Church drew near to the state and took upon itself the responsibility for the latter's destiny. This rapprochement made a place for the Emperor in the Church. When he became a Christian sovereign, the Church poured out its gifts upon him, by means of unction. It loved the Anointed, not only as head of the state but as one who bore a special charism, the charism of rule, as the bridegroom of the Church, possessing the image of Christ himself. The Emperor received a special place in the hierarchy. It is difficult to determine exactly what that place was, for the imperial function had many meanings. On the one hand, the Emperor was venerated as the bearer of a special charism; on the other, he represented, in the Church, the people, the laity, the elect nation, the "royal priesthood." Finally, as holder of power, he was the first servant of the Church; in his person the state was crowned by the Cross. Constantine the Great himself defined this function as "bishop for external affairs." He here returned to the title of bishop the meaning of watching over the financial and administrative affairs of the community which it had in the time of the Apostles. The influence of the Emperor in the Church was measured in fact by his power in the state. Owing to his position as "bishop for external affairs" he could exercise a great influence over the Church; he even convoked and presided at ecumenical councils, a fact never objected to in the East or West.

The relationship between Church and state was established in principle on the pattern of a "symphony," that is mutual harmony and independence of the two parts. The state recognized the ecclesiastical law as an interior guide for its activity; the Church considered itself as under the state. This was not a Caesaro-papism in which the ecclesiastical supremacy belonged to the Emperor. Caesaro-papism was always an abuse; never was it recognized, dogmatically or canonically. The "symphonic" relations between Church and state ended in the Emperor's directing all the domain of ecclesiastical life and legislation within the limits of his administration of the state. But, if that "symphony" became troubled by discord, if the Emperors attempted to impose on the Church dogmatic directions, which sometimes were heresies (Arianism, Iconoclasm), then the Church thought itself persecuted, and the real nature of its connection with the state became manifest, for Caesaro-papism was never a dogma. Still, the Church attached much importance to its alliance with the state, in so far as state was of use to Church and as the existence of a crowned head for the entire Orthodox world—the Orthodox Emperor—was considered one of the Church's essential attributes. The Emperor was the sign of the conquest of the world by the Cross; he was the "architect" of the Kingdom of God on earth.

At the time of the fall of Byzantium, the Orthodox Emperor was succeeded by the Russian Tsar, who had put on the Byzantine crown and considered himself as the direct successor of the Orthodox Empire. In Russia, in modern times, the concept of the Tsar was not so simple and so logical as in Byzantium. Beginning with the time of Peter the Great this idea was complicated with Lutheran elements of the supremacy of the monarch in the Church, and this principle, false and inadmissible for the Church, penetrated— although with certain necessary restrictions—into the fundamental laws of the state, although it was never proclaimed as a law of the Church. Here certain elements of Caesaro-Papism crept in as abuses, the idea of the Orthodox Emperor and of his place in the Church remained what it was of old, and had nothing in common with a papism personified in the Emperor (Caesaro-papism). The Orthodox Church always wished to influence the power of the state as much as possible, but from within and not from without. The Roman theory of two powers, according to which the Pope instituted monarchs by anointing and deposed them by excommunication—according to which he was thus supreme dispenser of all political authority—has never existed in Orthodoxy.

When, in the person of the Emperor Constantine, glorifed by the Church as "equal to the Apostles," the state became Christian, it might seem that the question of the relations between Church and state was decided. The state ceased to be "the beast," lost its pagan nature, entered into the Kingdom of God. At the same time the problem of the hieratic position of the Emperor was solved; the imperial person entered the ecclesiastical hierarchy as the anointed of God. The relations between the Emperor and the episcopate and the place of the Emperor in the Church seemed as fixed as the unmovable foundations of the latter. But events have shown such a conclusion to be false; the Orthodox Church has twice lost its Orthodox Emperor, once by the fall of Byzantium and again, in our day, by the fall of the Russian Empire. Under these circumstances it has returned to the state of things which existed before Constantine. (The sovereigns of the Balkan states cannot be considered as heads of Orthodox empires equal to those of Byzantium and Russia).

The Church now exists without an Emperor, but its charismatic situation, the plenitude of its gifts, has not changed because of this. What then has happened? In reality, it was not so simple and so easy as might be thought to transform a pagan into a Christian state. It was easy, by the Edict of Milan, to change a persecuted religion into a tolerated religion, and later into the religion of the state and even to put on it an official dress. But the life of the state itself remained pagan from top to bottom: it remained impregnated with concepts of the Roman Empire and of oriental despotism. Byzantium—in the person of its Emperors—made considerable efforts to bring the laws of the state into accord with those of the Church, but that was only the beginning of a long historic journey, interrupted by catastrophe. The same thing happened in Russia. In the old Russia there were many beautiful traits of patriarchal piety, but there were also so many natural and pagan elements, and in the Russian state so many elements of Prussian and Asiatic despotism, that it would have been premature to speak of a Christian state. This was the condition of the whole Christian world, in the West too, which was raised from primitive barbarism to Christianity. The situation of the Orthodox Empire—Byzantine and Russian—was not different from that of the Germanic Holy Roman Empire. The Christian Empires were only a symbol of what ought to be, and it would certainly be a grave error to identify the symbol or the dream with reality. Christian Emperors lead their peoples toward the Christ as far as such an orientation was possible. But this time is past, for life itself has put an end to any real representation of the people of the Church in the person of the prince, a representation which was the basis for the Emperor's authority in the Church. In this representation the power of the prince has become a fiction which leads to the worst forms of tyranny—ecclesiastical tyranny and the yoke of Caesaro-papism. The people have begun their own life, apart from such representation of the people by the prince. And now if the state can be penetrated by the spirit of the Church, it must be from within, not from without, not from above but from below.

We come, then, to a new aspect of the relations between Church and state, an aspect belonging to our own times. Here we have two questions to consider: one concerning the relations between Orthodoxy and the imperial power, and another touching the relations of Orthodoxy with the state in general. Is the connection between Orthodoxy and the imperial power (''autocracy'') dogmatically determined? Or is it not an accidental connection, formed in the course of history, which history has now abolished? In the long centuries of the existence of the Orthodox Empire, the established order was considered immovable. This conviction never became a dogma, and could not become one, simply because it had no foundations in Christianity. As I have already said, the Emperor, God's anointed, the bearer of the charism of power, the representative of the laity, occupied a certain place in the Church. But that place is not essential to the existence of the Church as is the hierchy of the apostolic succession—the clergy and the episcopate. On the other hand, the laity, the people of God, the ''royal priesthood,'' is as necessary to the Church as the hierarchy: the pastors cannot exist without the flock. But this importance of the laity cannot be allied to their representation in the person of the Emperor; it is thoroughly possible now, as it was in the primitive Church for the people to have no personal representative. It is true that the idea of a king in the person of Christ is inherent in the Church. This is not a political idea, connected with a certain form of state organization, but an idea wholly religious. This idea may be realized in a democracy, by an elected representative of power, a president, quite as well as by an autocrat. It is, in general, the idea of the sanctification of power in the person of its supreme representative. It is the idea of the holy king, indicated beforehand in the Old Testament (psalms and prophetic books) and symbolized in the image of the ''meek king'' making his entry into the royal city. It is allied to the promise ''of the reign of the Saints with Christ,'' at the first resurrection, of which the Apocalypse speaks (ch.20). As a matter of history, the imperial power strove to realize that idea, but instead denatured and obscured it. Perhaps it perished just because it did not conform interiorly to the idea of the sanctification of power.

This apocalypse of power is an Orthodox "utopia," a utopia founded on prophecies of a "white tsar," of a holy king, who would realize the Kingdom of God on earth. Here we have the transfiguration of power, power which is no longer the power of the sword, but that of love.

This ideology of the individual sanctification of power has nothing in common with any particular sort of political regime, especially with bureaucratic monarchy. Such a confusion of ideas has often occurred, and certain political groups, for whom religion is—consciously or not—a political instrument, perpetuate the notion, even today. To establish a connection between Orthodoxy, the religion of liberty, and reactionary political tendencies is a crying contradiction that may be explained by history but not by Orthodox dogma. True it is that, for long centuries, Orthodoxy was allied with monarchy; the latter rendered it many services, at the same time inflicting grave wounds. The "Christian state," while assuring the Orthodox Church a "dominant" situation, was at the same time an impediment, an historic obstacle to its free development. The tragedy of historic Orthodoxy, the fall of Byzantium, the condition of Russia in our time, may be explained in part by this lack of equilibrium between the Church and the state. It is false to transform the history of the Orthodox Empire, which has its dark as well as its light sides, into an apocalypse glorifying the past; it is false to see in that past a lost paradise, the Kingdom of God on earth. At the price of unnumbered victims the revolution has freed Orthodoxy forever from too close connection with the monarchial system. This connection, to tell the truth, was never of exclusive importance. The Orthodox Church has existed in various countries under different political regimes: in the republics of Novgorod and Pskov, as well as under the despotism of Ivan the Terrible, and under heterodox governments; never has it lost its fullness and its power. Today the Church exists under the yoke of Communism, and in the emigration, and in the entire world, independent of political conditions. There is no interior and immovable connection between Orthodoxy and this or that system of government; the Orthodox may have different opinions and different political sympathies. This is a matter of their consciences as citizens and of their intelligence. In certain circumstances, it is true, religious unity engenders uniformity of political ideas; this derives in part from the love which unites members of the Church, but, we repeat, there is no dogmatic connection between Orthodoxy and a predetermined political system. Orthodoxy is free and must not serve any political regime. Its ideal of the sanctification of power is religious, not political. And this is not the ideal of the two swords, or that of an ecclesiastical state such as a pontifical monarchy which Catholicism still does not wish to renounce. Orthodoxy admits neither papal-Caesarism nor Caesaro-papism.

The relations between Church and state have changed much in the course of history. Up to the revolution they were reduced to different forms of the "Christian state" in union with the Church. For a long time before the revolution the system of a state religion did not agree with the facts, for the modern state includes people of different confessions and even of different faiths. At present such a system (a state Church) has become wholly inapplicable. A division has been made between Church and state, advantageous to both. Separation of Church and state, under different forms, has replaced the ancient alliance.

This separation, at first imposed by force, has been accepted by the Orthodox Church also, for it corresponds with its dignity and its vocation. In certain countries, the separation has not been completely effected, but even here the situation of the Orthodox Church is quite different from what it once was as a state Church. Since Orthodoxy has ceased to be a state Church, it has lost a situation to which various advantages are attached, but which also carried a heavy burden. The established Church of England is a good example of both. In fact, the separation of Church and state may have implications ranging all the way from that of direct persecution (Soviet Russia) to that of complete liberty of conscience (United States). (The Soviet government, by the way, although it proclaimed "de-jure" the separation of Church and state, is "de facto" the only truly "confessional state" in the world. Here the dominant religion is the militant atheism of the Communist sects. Other religions are no longer tolerated.) The liberty we find in the United States is now the regime most favorable to the Church, most normal for it; it frees the Church from the temptations of clericalism, and assures it development without hindrance. Doubtless this system is valid only provisionally, depending upon its historic usefulness.

But the Church in accepting juridical separation from Caesar, from the state, and in seeing it as liberation, does not renounce its influence over the whole of life. The ideal of the transformation of the state by the interior energies of the Church remains in all its force and without any restriction, at the very time of separation of Church and state; for that separation remains exterior and not interior. The Church's methods of influence change; the work is no longer done outside, from above, but from within, from below, from the people and by the people. The representation of the people by the Christian sovereign, in force at the time of the Orthodox Empire, no longer exists; the laity participate in the life of the Church, without any intermediary, so that the Church influences the state in a democratic way. But it is a democracy of souls. New dangers, new difficulties arise in this way, analogous to those which existed at the time of the alliance between Church and state. The Church may be led to interfere in party politics; the latter, in its turn, may divert the Church from its true path. But an essential advantage remains; the Church exercises its influence on souls by the way of liberty, which alone corresponds to Christian dignity, not by that of constraint. Constraint leads more quickly to certain results, but it carries with it its own punishment. Contemporary history in both East and West proves this. We cannot close our eyes to the less desirable results of the separation of Church and state; in our time when personal liberty is more and more disregarded, the separation often becomes direct or indirect violation of the rights of the Church, extending even to persecution. But we must have faith that, in spite of these trials, Providence is leading the Church to free itself from heterogenous, parasitic formations which have invaded its body during the centuries. The ultimate influence of the Church on life, and especially on the state, will be only increased by separation of Church and state.

CHAPTER 14

ORTHODOXY AND ECONOMIC LIFE

Religion, the predominant conception of the world, marks with its imprint the "economic man." An interior connection is established in the human soul between religion and economic activity. The process of bringing to light this connection is one of the most interesting pages of modern economic science. There exists, side by side with other spiritual types, a Christian type of the economic man, a general type and types peculiar to different confessions, Orthodox, Catholic, Protestant (with many branches, Puritan, Lutheran, Reformed, Quaker, etc.) Is it possible to establish the particular traits of the Orthodox economic man? Let us note first the economic traits proper to all Christianity, then those specifically inherent in Orthodoxy in its concrete historic circumstances.

The political economy of contemporary Europe is now developed on the basis of science, which often seems a strange and hostile element to Christianity, but is actually born of it. It is the creation of Christian man, freed from nature and its dominance, which held pagan man prisoner. Man has understood that he is the master and the center of nature. This is only an indirect result of Christianity, for, in being not of this world, or even above it, Christianity gives man the realization of his own power and spirituality. And, free in spirit, he feels his vocation, which is to realize what his will and his intelligence can accomplish in the world. Slowly, but inevitably, there begins for European peoples "modern history," the epoch of Humanism, of the Renaissance, and later the epoch of Industrialism which is perhaps only at the beginning of its route. Our time is unconscious of its historic and spiritual influences; it inclines rather to the side of paganism, but in truth it is born of the Christian spirit.

One condition of economic energy is recognition of the natural world as good and valuable: more, even, the recognition of a certain kinship between man and the world. This is especially noticeable if one thinks of Buddhism's renunciation of the world and its pessimistic idea of the world as a place of suffering and illusion. It is evident that such a point of view paralyses the economic will. There are two ways of accepting the world: (1) a natural, pagan way; man remains the victim of natural forces, deified by him. He cannot free himself from orgiastic drunkeness, from a slavish attitude towards the nature he adores (such are all pagan religions, Egyptian, Hellenic, Babylonian, etc.); (2) a Christian way; man "accepts" the world as the creation of God. Man is the chief of the creation; he accepts it with love, but also with the feeling of his own independence, proper to a being conscious of his spirituality. Man is superior to nature, but he is at the same time a natural being. This is the fact which establishes a positive relation between man and nature, that garden of God which man is called to cultivate and where he should command. We see here a sort of antinomy; on the one hand Christianity calls man to free himself from the world, from love of the world, from all economic care. "Consider the birds of the air; they sow not, neither do they reap, nor gather into barns, and your Heavenly Father feedeth them" (Matt. 6:26). "Those who buy should be as those who possess not, etc." (1 Cor. 7:30-1). Thus Christianity establishes an ascetic opposition in regard to the world. But at the same time only Christianity teaches us to love the world with a supreme love, this world which is the creation of God, which God so loved that He not only created it by His wisdom but spared not His Own Son to save it. The world is made eternal by God, or the actual nature of the world must change and give place to a new heaven and new earth. In Christianity man is not only the intellectual logos, but also the economic logos of the world, the master of creation. His is the right and the duty to work in the world for his own existence (2 Thess. 3:10), to aid his neighbor and to accomplish the common work of humanity (Matt 25:), in accordance with the precepts of God: "Subdue the earth and rule over it" (Gen. 1:28). The work of man is a part of his connection with nature and to it the sanctifying grace of the Holy Spirit is joined.

This abiding of the Holy Spirit in the world, through the Church, is expressed in the many things blessed by the Church—food, vessels, etc. In principle everything may be holy except those things employed with evil intention.

The sanctification of things needful to man and used by man is, in principle, of great importance; these are above all the materials necessary to the administration of the sacraments, the Eucharistic bread and wine, the chrism for Chrismation, and the oil for unction of the sick, the waters for Baptism. Afterward comes the sanctification (by blessing) of wine, bread, fruits, oil, honey grain, different objects, building, roads, etc. The Church thus gives its benediction to the natural elements. This benediction extends to the entire domain of economic production and consumption. The sanctification includes transfiguring power, so that man's activity which transforms nature, his economic toil, and the power of God which transfigures that nature, working above human power but not outside it, are wholly reunited.

All that has been said above determines the Orthodox point of view on economic life; we know that the history of Christianity always balances between two extremes: the renunciation of the world, and the acceptance of time. It is indisputable that Christianity has freed and rehabilitated all labor, economic labor above all, and has given it a new soul. In Christianity is born a new economic man and new motives incite him to work. This motivation bears the mark of a union of the renunciation and the acceptance of the world, is the ethic of economic asceticism, and it is just this reunion of extremes, which gives, by its intensity, the greatest energy to ascetic work, religiously motivated. Free ascetic work is the economic and religious power which sustains the very foundations of European civilization. It is well known to what degree the monasteries helped to people the wooded and marshy spaces of Europe, how they were the organizing centres of spiritual and economic life. The idealist character of economic work, so different from the bestial egoism of the class-conflict preached in our day, was a powerful factor in economic development. In spite of the asceticism manifested by the desire to leave the world and to rise above it, by the tendency to voluntary poverty, in spite of this asceticism which is the soul of all monastic life, the victory of economic egoism is also possible. This produces secularism, from which is born the contemporary economic man with his over-simplified psychology of the economic egoist.

This was illustrated by the fact of the early hermits who, after founding their lonely monasteries, soon found themselves in the midst of settlements which, attracted by the life within, grew up around their walls. The seekers of solitude were forced to move farther into the wilderness, only to have the same process repeated. As in life in general, here spiritual power was reforged into material wealth: the spirit conquers the material. This ascetic and spiritual nature of economic work, so obscured that one is no longer conscious of it, exists even in our time. The discipline of work, which was learned in Christian asceticism, is still visible in European society.

The plan indicated, the "primitive accumulation" of economic energy by ascetic work, is applicable for all parts of the Christian world—East and West. The economic man of Christianity is characterized by his faith. This does not mean that man should be freed from exterior pressure of economic necessity—the apostles of Christ themselves had to practise their calling of fishermen, and St. Paul had to make tents—but, interiorly, this burden is borne for love of God, in the name of Christian obedience.

In Orthodox monasteries "obedience" is the term used for all sorts of work assigned to the monks by their superiors, all of which tasks are considered as equally done for the salvation of souls, according to the will of God. This religious approach defines the spiritual quality of the economic agent: he must accomplish his economic ministry with a feeling of his religious responsibility, whatever his social position. This ethic of labor cannot be replaced by any other, humanistic or communistic. Communism creates a new slavery for the people, with its forced labor, and liberty belongs only to one ruling class or one party. Economic science tells us that the work of slaves is much inferior to free labor, from the purely economic point of view. And free economic labor, as well as the discipline of work, is given only by Christianity. (It is noteworthy that in Russia the word for peasant—''krestianin''—means simply a Christian, ''Kristianin.'') Of course, other religions have also furnished religious motives for work, Judaism, Islam, and even pagan religions. It is clear, for example, that the temples and pyramids of Egypt would never have been built by slavish compulsion alone, without a belief in God and immortality. But a free moral personality is developed only in Christianity: Christianity liberates economic energy, dissipating the nightmares of paganism, and at the same time directing that energy, regulating it from an ethical point of view.

During the centuries of Orthodox history, among oriental peoples, the agrarian economy predominated over industrial and financial capitalism. Like the Western Church, the Eastern disavowed the taking of interest, considered as usury. It is true that Byzantium knew no direct prohibition of interest taking, as was the case in the Catholic Church; it was not necessary to abolish canons to admit interest as a normal economic relation. Agricultural life, in accordance with the peculiarities of national character, of climate, of nature, etc., received the imprint of the Christian cult; that is clear if we consider the feasts, the blessings, the adaptation of different economic acts to the commemoration of the Saints. It cannot be denied that as a result of this there grew up, in certain places, what might be called agricultural religions somewhat resembling those of antiquity, e.g. the Athenian. But this is only a superficial resemblance. This ''agricultural religion'' carries into economic life much of radiance, of warmth, and of religious poetry, for it liberates the latter from the mechanical prose, so characteristic of the factory. In general, agricultural work is more favorable to religious life than that of factory or the city. Nevertheless the development of economic forms is a regular process, which it is not in human power to stop. This is the Orthodox view on the subject of industrialism, of contemporary urbanism, and on industrial capitalism in general.

If it is not possible to suppress it, because it is economically inevitable, it must be given a Christian meaning and ennobled. Instead of organizing exploitation, it is a question of organizing the work of all mankind so that it will serve its own supreme ends, those of Christian love rather than those of luxury and cupidity. From this comes a new purpose for Orthodoxy: the preaching of social Christianity. But has economic life a general eschatological meaning apart from the acquisition of daily bread? Do the results brought about by this life have a share in the salvation of the world? What is the meaning of economic and technical progress? Historic Orthodoxy has not yet studied these questions, which are only objects of contemporary theological speculation. The essential themes of that speculation may be summed up somewhat as follows: man is an economic agent not only in his quality as an individual, but also as a generic being. It may be said that economic action is accomplished not by an individual, but by all humanity, and the efforts and the results separately acquired lead to the domination of man over nature.

Man realizes his destiny—to be master of the universe, to reveal the energy of the world and to subdue it to his will. The common work of humanity is accomplished by means of economic labor. The Russian thinker N.F. Fedorov made this thought the center of his theological system. Economic activity brings to light the cosmic quality of man, his vocation, his power as a cosmic agent. In the economic domain, man lives the same life as that of the world, in all that concerns consumption and production. By consumption, especially by the action of eating, by "an exchange of matter," man realizes his union with the flesh of the world. The matter of this world, absorbed by man, becomes the elements of his body, and inversely these elements return again to the state of matter. This cycle testifies to the cosmic character of the body. Thus the body extends itself beyond its own immediate limits. Nourishment is our natural communion with the flesh of the world under the form of food. The other aspects of consumption (clothing, satisfactions for the needs of hearing, sight, touch, smell and all the senses) also lead to the humanization of matter, to the enlarging of the organs of the human body beyond its natural limits, and, in a sense, to the transformation of the matter of the world into a body belonging to all men. Besides, to work is actively to emerge from oneself, to go into the world. Every act of labor is a realization of the design for man outside himself. In labor he becomes not only the Logos of the world, but one of its workers.

In that which concerns the moralization of economic life, the influence of the Church is manifested by the education of ''spiritual taste,'' by the struggle against contemporary paganism, against luxury and perversity. It is difficult to measure the degree of that influence, but it is also difficult to deny it. Concerning distribution, the Church is called to be a social conscience which should raise its voice, speaking to the hearts of men and mingling in their public life.

For answering modern social questions, Orthodoxy has less historical experience than the Western Churches; they have to do with an industrial capitalism already developed, while Orthodox countries are still in a state of natural economy where agriculture predominates. But the questions raised in our day by Bolshevism are bringing the Church to attempt to solve this acute social problem.

We can thus point out the characteristic traits of Orthodoxy which bear upon the solution of the social problem. Let us note at once that Orthodoxy admits the hierarchy, but not clericalism; the spirit of Orthodoxy is ''conciliar.'' This spirit applied to social relations is what is called democracy. Certainly the ''conciliarity,'' ''sobornost,'' of Orthodoxy is not democracy, but the absence of princes of the Church and of an ecclesiastical monarch—the Pope—makes it of the people, favorable to the spirit of economic democracy. Dostoevsky said somewhere: ''Orthodoxy is our Russian socialism.'' He meant to say that in Orthodoxy we had the inspiration to love and to social equality lacking in atheist socialism. Orthodoxy was not only an imperial, but it draws nearer to the working classes. As to socialism, Orthodoxy—like Christianity in

—cannot traffic with atheism, which constitutes a sort of religion of socialism. The connection we observe today between socialism and anti-Christian "anthropotheism" is due to spiritual and historic causes. This is the "temptation of bread": humanity abjures the Christ and professes that man lives by bread alone (economic materialism). This sad fact, however, does not mean that the tie between socialism and atheism is indissoluble; another future, a Christian future, may be awaited. For the human soul is naturally Christian and cannot be satisfied by bread alone.

What is then, the Orthodox viewpoint on socialism? As yet, there has been no doctrinal deliverance on the subject, although such a definition is not indispensable, since it is not a dogmatic, but an ethical, a social question. Nevertheless, Orthodox tradition, the works of the Fathers of the Church (Basil the Great, St. John Chrysostom and others) offer us sufficient basis for accepting socialism in a general sense, that is to say, as the negation of the system of exploitation, of speculation, of cupidity. Orthodoxy should not oppose socialism if the latter recognizes the individual liberty; quite the contrary, for socialism is the realization in social life of the commandment of love. The Orthodox Church possesses enough power to respond to its social vocation—it can brighten with its light the way followed by humanity, it can awake the social conscience, it can annouce the good news to those who are burdened and heavy laden.

Because of its historic experience, Orthodoxy has always had less occasion to define its attitude towards social questions than had the Churches of the West. But just now, in Bolshevist Russia, the Orthodox Church is brought face to face with the social problem. When the iron grasp of godless Communism, which would strangle all life, finally relaxes, the Russian Chuch will not fail to apply, in the realm of social Christianity, the lessons it has learned in the present time of spiritual testing. During all the centuries of the existence of the Christian Church, and above all in the nineteenth century, many attempts were made to preach Christian socialism in the East as in the West. It is not enough that Christianity adapt itself to the changes in life which take place without its cooperation. Christianity is called to lead the people, to awaken their conscience, to lead them to make efforts toward new ends. In other words, we hope for the awakening of a new prophetic spirit in Christianity of which we saw the first indications in the Russian Orthodoxy of the nineteenth century. We hope that this spirit will develop more and more in Russia after the end of Bolshevism. Here is a problem much more important than the "Christian socialism" which, under different forms, we find in many countries. It concerned a new aspect of Christianity, its social aspect, a new form of the spirit of the Church, and of the creative work of the Church, an aspect universal and social, and what is now called socialism is only one of the exterior details which are but a prototype of the abundance of gifts which fill the Church. Christianity, too, has a social and communist "Utopia" which will come to pass on earth, and its name, according to the prophecies of the Old and New Testament, is the Kingdom of God; it belongs in its plenitude to the age to come, but it will be manifest on this earth, as testimony to the truth. The prophets of the Old Testament (Isaiah and others) testify to it, as well as the Apocalypse (ch. 20). Christ is a king and His kingdom, while not of this world, is being realized here below. The royal charism which He gave to the Church calls it to share in historical creativeness. May those who have ears to hear listen, now, to the rolling thunder of history.

Nevertheless, all this belongs to a future which is yet beyond the historic horizon. What is important for the moment is to make clear the Orthodox point of view on the subject of existing social classes and their reciprocal relations. It is very certain that Orthodoxy cannot be allied to any existing "class"—such as "the left" and "the right" would impose. Christianity is above limited and egotistical class distinctions. Neither can Orthodoxy be allied to any system of economic organization; these systems have each their turn in history. But in speaking of our epoch two principles may be established, sufficiently self-evident from the ethical and social view point. First, Orthodoxy does not mount guard over private property. Private property is an historic institution whose forms, as well as its social importance, are constantly changing; it has no enduring intrinsic value. Second, Orthodoxy cannot defend the capitalist system, for it is founded on the exploitation of hired labor. It can only traffic provisionally with the system, in view of its temporary merits. The capitalist system has augmented the productivity of labor and creative energy: that is good. But there are very clear limits to this good, and, consequently, to the extent of the Church's cooperation. Christianity cannot and should not compromise with Black slavery, nor with the exploitation of child labor, practised by capitalism in its beginnings. Besides, capitalism, like private property, is constantly changing its historic aspect, as it is penetrated, little by little, by certain elements of socialism, so that the abstract categories of capitalism and socialism, so useful for the demagogue, become totally inapplicable as soon as they are profoundly studied in the light of our conscience. There is only one supreme value in the light of which economic forces must be judged. That is freedom of personality, in law and in economy. Then the best economic form—whatever its name, and however it combines capitalism and socialism—is that which, in any given circumstances, best assures personal liberty, protecting it from natural poverty and social slavery. This is why the Orthodox viewpoint, on the subject of economic forms, takes history into account, first of all. It is the domain of relativism of methods; only the end remains unchangeable.[1]

Hence it can have only a negative attitude towards the Russian communism of today: in spite of certain social achievements communism does tyrannical violence to personal liberty; it is a direct denial of freedom of personality. It is a system of spiritual slavery, hence blasphemy against the Holy Spirit. It is not by accident that communism in Russia is accompanied by satanic hatred of God and His sanctuaries.

---

[1]On the general meaning of the economic life, see my book: *The Philosphy of Economics* (Russian).

CHAPTER 15

ORTHODOXY AND
APOCALYPTIC THOUGHT

The Bible includes an Apocalpse—not only that of St. John, which forms such a majestic end to the New Testament, but a whole series of Apocalypses: those of the prophetic books of the Old Testament, those of the Gospel (the words of Our Lord Himself), and those of the apostolic writings. These Apocalypses testify to the tragedy of the world and of human history, to the tragic destiny of the Church, the trials it has to face. But they concern not only the question of trials, of the agony of the world before its end, but also the future of the Church yet awaiting its accomplishment. Is there a future in the life of the Church, a fullness of time, which includes a new creation, a new prophecy, a new inspiration: a future which will not be entirely new, for it will be made manifest within the limits of the Church, of the New Testament, in its heart, but which will add new elements, as yet unknown, in history? Or may it not be in principle that there is nothing new in Church history, this new future having already occurred in the inmost life of the Church? The phenomenon persists, but it is really an epilogue which may extend to several more acts.

There may be three answers to these questions; the first is that of the primitive Christians. According to that answer there is no future, for there is no remaining time; the last hour of history has sounded. The second coming of Our Lord must be immediately expected. In such a reply the Apocalyptic ideas are swallowed up by eschatology. There is another response to this question: the history of the Church is interiorly finished, but is prolonged exteriorly; the Church already possesses the plenitude of all it should bring to pass. Then, fundamentally, nothing separates us from the end, there is only the question of duration of time, and not that of new elements in its achievement. This conception holds that a third revelation following the second one, at Pentecost, is impossible: that the whole truth has already been revealed although new aspects of it may yet be noted. This view is more naturally accepted by Catholicism, which has in the papacy a finished dome which, although it completes the Church building, yet hides the stars. For Catholicism, the papacy is past, present and future, so complete that it need seek nothing new. This interpretation does not sufficiently take into consideration the apocalyptic texts, so brilliant in clarity and power. For a long time Orthodoxy also accepted this concept, partly under the influence of Catholic thought, partly in conformity with the spirit of the epoch. The Byzantine Church, especially, could feel itself as immovable and definitely established under the protection of imperial power as the Western Church under the Pope; it was only after the fall of Byzantium that the relative and conditional character of the epoch clearly appeared.

Notwithstanding the spiritual interpretation of the Apocalypse by the hierarchy, the soul of Russian Orthodoxy is, in its depth, always open to the emotion and the presentiment of apocalyptic concepts noted above. The Russian Apocalypse has two aspects, just as have the apocalyptic prophecies themselves: a sad aspect and a joyous. In the first case it is the sad side of apocalyptic tragedies which receives chief emphasis, an eschatological meaning. The annunciation of the coming end of the world assumes prime importance, and this sometimes results in a spiritual "evasion," a panic flight; to seek an asylum in eschatology, there is a flight from life itself. This panic is felt strongly in the schism of the Russian Old Believers. The Old Believers separated themselves from the official Church, but their spiritual life has perceived and preserves the spirit of the Orthodox Church, though in a certain inevitably narrow way. The appearance of an Anti-Christ—the Emperor Peter the Great—the interruption of the priestly succession by "heresy," finally the mark of the beast, imposed on all atheist states, such were, in the eyes of the Old Believers, the signs of the approaching end of the world. The more zealous fled into the forests and burned themselves, preferring a baptism of fire to life under the yoke of Anti-Christ. But side by side with these sombre ideas there is the legend of the shining city of

Kitezh—a city submerged by Divine will at the bottom of the lake, but remaining intact and even visible to worthy eyes. This eschatological state of soul exists up to the present time, even when Russian people are truly under the yoke of "the beast who speaks blasphemous words against God and everything holy." By the side of this popular eschatology, other apocalyptic hopes were reborn during the nineteenth century among the religious intellectuals; new perspectives appear, still unexplored in the life of the Church. These apocalyptic hopes remain confused and vague. They cannot, by their very character, be otherwise, for they concern what belongs to the realm of prophecy. So long as a developer has not been found, the images on a plate remain imperfectly understood, but the time must come when the prophecies will be manifest and accomplished. A common faith unites all those who have apocalyptic hopes and feelings. History has not yet arrived at its heart-breaking end; it is not yet interiorly finished, and the history of the Church contains a new future. In the face of this future, it seems, we should think not of the end, but rather of the beginning of history, the "fullness of time."

Historically, humanity understands this "fullness," each age according to its own degree of comprehension. The Orthodox conscience of our day understands it under the maximal form, as the penetration of all life by the influences of the Church. At a time when the separation of Church and state has become the common rule, this idea may seem Utopian and outworn. But it could have been arrived at only in the moment when the submission of Church to state, interior and exterior, amounting sometimes to slavery, had come to an end. This submission was once considered as a rule for the reciprocal relations of Church and state, and was called "The Christian State." Having renounced that idea, Orthodoxy can finally face the problem of the interior regeneration of the state. Is not this the idea which, among others, is contained in the prophecy of the coming of the millennium, in chapter 20 of the Apocalypse? Surely, that task presupposes new powers to be discovered in the Church.

Christianity discovers another, similar task for itself, in its attitude toward and influence upon culture. "Culture" comes from the "cult" and thus partakes of the nature of the mysteries of the theurgical. But culture has been secularized, separated from the Church, so that the Church has now been relegated to a position where it is considered simply as one department of culture. But the original idea is the true one, the present attitude an aberration which must be cured. This is indicated by the fact that the deepest of modern scientific studies, in any given phase of thought, art or science, or what not, always seem to bring the investigators back to the idea of God.

The life of the Church should attain a plenitude as yet unknown. Up to the present, personal salvation has been the center of its life, but in the future the Church must reveal the forces of Christian public life, it must not capitulate before the secularization already accomplished, and the rising flood of atheism. This is the belief of modern Russian apocalyptic thought. All the present is only a dialectic moment in historical development, an antithesis, which should be followed by a new synthesis. The history of the Church has still a future; there are still problems to be solved. If the green tree of Christianity now seems withered, is it not just because the Gardener has cut the dead branches, so that new ones may grow more vigorously?

This idea of a supreme vocation for the Church and its ministry in the world animates, under different forms, most of the Russian thinkers of the nineteenth and twentieth centuries. This same idea forms the ideological basis of the Orthodox Russian Student Christian movement abroad. Different thinkers have given different interpretations to the idea, but the problems remain practically the same in every case. Their common appeal is to the spirit of creation, to inspiration, to the transfiguration of life. (In the doctrine of N. Fedorov, mentioned above, we find more than that, an appeal to the resurrection of the fathers by the children which effaces the limits between present and future and the limits between the Apocalypse and eschatology.) All these creative aspirations may seem to be the

fantasies of isolated thinkers, without historical basis, without foundation in the life of the Church. This is not the case; they all come
from the one spirit of the Orthodox Church and are nourished at its
subterranean sources. Were not the prophets of Israel, when they
foresaw the future beyond the destruction of kingdoms and of
worlds, held by their contemporaries to be dreamers of this kind?
For this glow of Orthodox thought, for these creative appeals, there
is an interior evidence stronger than anything exterior. In any case
man should not try to limit or change the meaning of the Lord's
Prayer: ''Thy Kingdom come, Thy will be done on earth as it is in
Heaven.''

CHAPTER 16

ORTHODOX ESCHATOLOGY

"I look for the resurrection of the dead and the life of the world to come." This is the last article of the Creed, and this is the belief of all Christians. The present life is the road which leads to eternity: "the reign of grace" transformed into "The fashion of this world passes" (I Cor. 7:31), moving towards its end. All Christian perception of the present world is determined by this eschatology; it does not deprive this life of its value, but the perception receives a new supreme justification. Primitive Christianity is quite full of the sentiment of a near and inevitable end. "Yea, I come soon. Amen. Come, Lord Jesus" (Rev. 22:20). These words of fire resounded like celestial music in the hearts of primitive Christians and made them, we may say, "super-terrestrial." That expectation of an immediate end, that joyous tension, naturally disappear in the course of history. This idea has been replaced by that of quick termination of our life by death and of the retribution to come afterwards; in the East and West eschatology has become more severe and somber. At the same time there has developed in Christianity—in Orthodoxy especially—a special veneration for death, in some points quite near to the ideas of ancient Egypt (in general there exists a sort of "subterranean" connection between Egyptian piety in the pagan world and Orthodox among Christians). The dead body is interred with veneration as the seed of the coming resurrection, and the very ritual of inhumation is held by certain ancient writers to be a sacrament. Prayer for the dead, periodic commemoration of the departed establishes a connection between us and the other world. In liturgical language, every dead body is called a "relic," for it is capable of being glorified.

The separation of soul and body is a sort of sacrament where at the same time the judgment of God is delivered upon the fallen Adam. The man finds himself torn by the unnatural disjunction of soul and body, but at the same time the soul is born anew, in the spiritual world. The soul separated from the body becomes conscious of its spirituality and finds itself in the world of incorporeal spirits—spirits both luminous and dark. In this new estate, the soul must find itself in relation to the new world. In other words, the state of the soul must be made manifest to the soul itself. The destinies of the soul are described by means of different images in ecclesiastical literature, but Orthodox doctrine speaks of them with a wise uncertainty, for it is a mystery not to be penetrated except in the living experience of the Church. Nevertheless, there is one axiom in the Church's consciousness: the worlds of the dead and of the living are separated, but the wall of separation is not unsurmountable by love and the power of prayer. Prayer for the dead, either in the course of the Eucharistic sacrifice, or outside the liturgy, occupies an important place in the Orthodox Church. The Church believes firmly in the real action of these prayers. They can ameliorate the state of the souls of sinners, and liberate them from the place of distress, and snatch them from hell. This action of prayer, of course, supposes not only intercession before the Creator, but a direct action on the soul, an awakening of the powers of the soul, capable of making it worthy of pardon.

The Orthodox Church recognizes two states in the world beyond the tomb: on the one hand, the beatitude of Paradise; on the other, a state of suffering. The Orthodox Church does not know purgatory as a special place or state. There are not sufficient biblical or dogmatic foundations for asserting the existence of a third place of this nature. Nevertheless, the possibility of a state of purification is undeniable—an idea common to both Orthodoxy and Catholicsm. From the point of view of practical religion, the distinction between hell and purgatory is imperceptible, for the fate of each soul beyond the tomb is completely unknown to us. What is fundamentally important is not the distinction between hell and purgatory as two different places where souls live; it is more their distinction as different states. This offers, consequently, the possibility of liberation from the pains of hell and of passing from an estate of reprobation to that of justification. In this sense it may be asked not if a purgatory exists, but even more if a "definitive hell" exists. In other words, is not hell a sort of purgatory? The Church at least knows no bounds to the efficacy of prayers for those who have quitted this world in union with the Church, and it believes in the effective action of these prayers.

Upon those who never belonged to the Church or have fallen away from it, the Church passes no judgment, but leaves them to the mercy of God. God has left us ignorant of the destinies of those who have not known Christ and have not entered into the Church. A certain hope is given us by the teaching of the Church on the descent of Christ into hell and His preaching on hell, addressed to all pre-Christian humanity. The word stands firm that God "wishes all men to be saved and to come to the knowledge of the truth" (I Tim. 2:4). Nevertheless, the Church has never officially defined the destiny of non-Christians, adult or infant.

An individual eschatology of death and of the world beyond the tomb has partially replaced the general eschatology of the second coming. From time to time the sentiment of waiting for the Christ Who comes, in the prayer: "Come, Lord Jesus," burns with a new flame in human souls and illumines them with a glimmer of another world. This feeling should never weaken in Christian hearts, for it is—in a certain sense—the measure of their love for Christ. Moreover, eschatology may have two aspects: one luminous, the other dark. The latter is sometimes due to terror and to religious panic, as when certain Russian Old Believers burned themselves to be saved from the reigning Anti-Christ. But eschatology can and should have a joyous aspect, turned towards the coming Christ. In the steady march of history we move gradually toward this meeting and the rays of light which brighten His second advent become visible. It may be that we have before us, just now, a new epoch in the life of the Church, illumined by these rays. The second coming of Christ is not only terrible for us (for He comes as Judge) but also glorious, for He comes in His Glory; and this glory is, at the same time, the glorification of the world and the fullness of all creation.

The glorified state, inherent in the body of the risen Christ, will be communicated to the whole of creation; a new heaven and a new earth will appear, a transfigured earth, resurrected with the Christ and His Humanity. All this will be connected with the resurrection of the dead performed by Christ through His angels. This "fullness of completion" is represented in Scripture symbolically in the images of the Jewish apocalypse. In one way or another death is vanquished, and all mankind, freed from the power of death, appears for the first time, entire and whole, forming a unity which is not weakened by the changing generations. Before the conscience of all mankind will be placed the problem of its common work in history. But at the same time this will be a judgment, the terrible judgment of Christ on humanity.

The Orthodox doctrine concerning the Last Judgment, in so far as it is revealed in scripture, is common to the whole Christian world. The last separation of the sheep and the goats, death and hell, damnation, eternal pain for some, the kingdom of heaven, eternal beatitude, the contemplation of Our Lord for others—this is the end of humanity's earthly road. A judgment presupposes not only the possiblity of justification but also that of condemnation; this is evident. Every man who confesses his sins knows that he deserves to be condemned of God: "If thou, Lord, shouldst mark iniquities, who could stand?" (Ps. 13:3). At the Last Judgment, when Our Lord Himself, meek and lowly of heart, will be the Judge of Truth, rendering justice in the name of the Father, how shall we find mercy? Orthodoxy responds to that question by iconography. Our icons of the Judgment represent the most pure Virgin at the right hand of the Son. She asks for mercy in the name of her maternal love, for she is the Mother of God and of the whole human race. When He received from the Father the Judgeship of truth (John 5:22 and 27), Our Lord confided pity to His Mother. But yet another mystery is revealed: the Mother of God, the "Pneumatophore, " is the living intermediary of the Holy Spirit, and through her the Holy Spirit shares in the Last Judgment. No man can be without sin: even among the sheep the taint of the other group remains in some degree. But the consoling Spirit heals and restores the sorely-wounded creature. He grants pardon by divine pity. Here we face a religious antinomy—condemnation and pardon—which testifies to the mystery of the divine will.

In Christian eschatology the question is always present of those sent into the eternal fire, prepared for the devil and his angels. From most ancient times doubts have existed as to the eternal duration of these torments; they are sometimes viewed as a provisional pedagogic method of influencing the soul, and a final restoration is hoped for. From earliest times there have been two tendencies in eschatology: the rigorist affirms that the suffering is eternal, definitive and without end; the other, which Augustine ironically calls the "pitiful" ("misericordes"), denies the eternity of punishment and the persistence of evil in creation, and proclaims the final victory of the Kingdom of God, when "God shall be all in all." The doctrine of the "restoration," is not only that of Origen, of whom Orthodoxy is doubtful because of certain of his opinions, but also of St. Gregory of Nyssa, glorified by the Church as Doctor, and his disciples. It has hitherto been thought that the doctrine of Origen was condemned at the fifth ecumenical council, but recent historical studies do not permit us to affirm this. As to the doctrines of St. Gregory, developed much later, and free from Origen's theories on the preexistence of souls, they have never been condemned. Consequently they have the right to be quoted in the Church, at least as theological opinions ("theologoumena"). It is true that the prevailing opinion among Orthodox dogmatic manuals does not go as far as the idea of the "restoration," sometimes even expressing ideas near to the rigor of Catholicism. On the other hand, certain thinkers have professed and still profess ideas influenced by the doctrine of St. Gregory of Nyssa, or, in any case, more complex than the ordinary rigorist view. It may thus be foreseen that this question will be restudied many times, and that it will eventually be made clear in new light sent to the Church by the Holy Spirit. In any case, no rigorist view can take from us the hope afforded in the triumphant words of St. Paul: "God has shut all men up in rebellion, that He might have mercy upon all. O the depth of the riches of the wisdom and of the knowledge of God'' (Rom. 11:32, 33).

CHAPTER 17

ORTHODOXY AND OTHER CHRISTIAN CONFESSIONS

All the foregoing may give some idea of the relationship between Orthodoxy and other Christian confessions. Note at once that the Orthodox Church is aware that she is the true Church, possessing the plenitude and purity of the truth in the Holy Spirit. Hence proceeds the attitude of the Orthodox Church toward other confessions, separated, immediately or not, from the unity of the Church; it can desire but one thing, that is to make Orthodox the entire Christian world, so that all confessions, may be grounded in universal Orthodoxy. This is not a spirit of proselytism or imperialism; it is the inherent logic of the situation, for the truth is one and cannot be measured by half-truths. Neither is it a mark of pride, for the guardianship of the truth is entrusted to a recipient, not for its merits, but by election, and the history of the chosen people, as well as that of Orthodoxy, shows that the guardians of the truth may be little worthy of their calling. But truth is inflexible and inexorable, and will not suffer compromise.

Thus the Christian world should become Orthodox; but just what does this mean? Does it mean that everyone should become a member of a certain church organization? Is it a conquest of ecclesiastical imperialism? There does not even exist in Orthodoxy a single ecclesiastical organization which could be entered; the Orthodox Church is a system of national, autocephalous Churches, allied one with another. It is true that individuals often join themselves to Orthodoxy by becoming members of one of the national Churches, but this fact offers no solution for the question of the relationship between ecclesistical communities or confessions. The only solution would be the following: these communities, while preserving intact their historical, national, and local characters, would draw near to Orthodox doctrine and life and would become capable of joining forces in the unity of the ecumenical Church, as

187

autonomous or autocephalous churches. Such an exterior reunion presupposes, of course, a corresponding interior movement. But such a movement is not impossible, for all ecclesiastical communities, even those whose road is farthest from that of the Orthodox Church, preserve a considerable part of the universal tradition, and, as a result of this, share in Orthodoxy. They all have "a grain" of Orthodoxy.

This Orthodox spirit, which lives in the universal Church, is more apparent to the eye of God than to that of man. In the first place all baptized persons are Christians, hence, in a certain sense, Orthodox. For Orthodoxy is composed, so to speak, of two circles: a large circle, the court of the temple, and a narrow circle, the temple itself and the holy of holies. Orthodoxy does not desire the submission of any person or group; it wishes to make each one understand. This is a field for the operation of the Holy Spirit which lives in the Church, beyond the direct efforts of men. Note here the sharp distinction between the attitude of Orthodoxy and that of Roman Catholicism. For the latter, reunion means, first of all, submission to the papal authority. Orthodoxy does not value exterior submission. And if such submission is necessary, it is only for the purpose of settling matters of the canonical organization of the community joining in ecumenical unity, or to guard against the ambitious pretensions of a local church, of which history affords examples. The ideal of the "union of the Churches" in its contemporary form would be realized by the entry of all Christian communities into the heart of Orthodoxy, but only if the maximum and not the minimum of the common heritage of the Churches forms the basis of reunion. By setting aside an abstract minimum on which all ecclesiastical societies would agree, unity could by no means be attained; this could only be the one first step on the road.

Only an agreement between the Churches, founded on the maximum of their common inheritance, can lead the Christian world to real union. This maximum is Orthodoxy. It cannot be a sort of amalgam or compromise, like a religious Esperanto, still less indifference to all dogmatic questions. Neither can it be something quite new in the history of the Church; then all the earlier life of the Church would have been a mistake, a misunderstanding, non-being. Orthodoxy is the interior way, the interior necessity for the universal Church on its way towards unity; it is only in Orthodoxy that the problems raised by the Christian confessions find a solution and an end, for it possesses the truth. Orthodoxy is not one of the historic confessions, it is the Church itself in its verity. It may even be added that, by becoming a confession, Orthodoxy fails to manifest all its force and its universal glory; it hides, one might say, in the catacombs.

The movement towards the reconstitution of universal Orthodoxy is steadily gaining force. In the same measure that the tendency of the sects toward isolation ceases, in the same measure that the ecumenical spirit is triumphing over sectarian phariseeism—this movement is pressing forward irresistibly, before our eyes today. It is not the result of Orthodox proselytizing, since there is no such thing. Contemporary Orthodoxy would probably not be able to muster strength sufficient for such a task, even if it wished. It is the Spirit of God Who leads the peoples toward Orthodoxy, in spite of human frailty and narrowness. As a matter of fact, what is the most important phenomenon of the spiritual life of the Christian world today? The search for the ecumenical Church, for integral unity. This unity may be realized only in two ways: by Orthodox conciliarity, "sobornost," or by the authoritarian monarchy of Catholicism. The success and the conquests of ecclesiastical authoritarianism may be considerable now, and perhaps even greater in the future. Still, it may confidently be affirmed that the conquest of the Christian world by a religion of authority is an aim which cannot hope to be realized; if that should happen it would be a proof of reaction and of spiritual decadence. The world will not become Catholic; on the other hand, we observe that papalism is becoming more and more isolated in the Christian world. This fact became very clear with the appearance of the encyclical "Mortalium Animos" after the Conference of Lausanne. It must be noted, however, that Catholicism is something greater than papalism. It may well be said that the Monarchy of the Vatican is a sort of shell, beneath which is the living body of the Church. And against the poisons of "statehood," of judicial authority, or ecclesiastical monarchy, which have affected that body, the everliving organism of the Church is constantly manufacturing anti-toxins. In spite of the triumph of authority in any Christian confession, the integral conscience of the ecumenical Church continues to live in the depths and naturally tends to another—an interior unity. This is witnessed by all the living holiness so plentiful in Catholicism, not because of papalism, but in spite of it. This is witnessed again by the purely religious movements in Catholicism, such as the liturgical movement among the Benedictines or the "Union" movement of the Priory of Amay (Belgium).

The same tendency is much more clearly evident in the Protestant world. The two names of Stockholm and Lausanne symbolize the movement toward reunion, which has begun in the heart of the Christian world, and which is already bearing fruit. But this movement brings with it a reexamination and revaluation of the spiritual basis of the Christian communities. By the very force of circumstances, it leads irresistibly to more profound consideration of questions concerning ecclesiastical tradition, and in consequence, it leads to a return, at first almost imperceptible, towards Orthodoxy. This return is already evident in the advanced movements of the Protestant world, which designate themselves as "Hochkirchliche Bewegung." Thanks to the modern tendency to restore the plenitude of tradition, thanks to certain movements which are leading to the liberation of Catholicism from the Roman system, an important rapprochement in regard to Orthodoxy is becoming outlined. But the decisive act, perhaps still far distant, would consist in the reestablishment of the hierarchy of the Apostolic Succession in those bodies where it was abolished.

A special place in this movement is occupied by the Episcopal Church of England, America and other countries. I shall not touch, here, the subject of the validity of Anglican orders, merely a canonical and not a dogmatic question, which can be decided for the

Orthodox Church only by a competent ecclesiastical authority. In any case, the Episcopal Church is, of all the Protestant world, the nearest to Orthodoxy. Among the many tendencies in Anglicanism the Anglo-Catholic movement becomes more and more important; it is persistently devoted to reestablishment of ancient tradition and thus flows into the stream of Orthodoxy. We may hope that the reunion of Orthodoxy and of the Episcopal Churches of England and America will be an accomplishment of the not too distant future, and that this movement will be a decisive phase in the reestablishment of the unity lost to the Church, and of peace between the East and the West.

The Orthodox Church takes part in the inter-confessional, "ecumenical" movements of our day in which Catholicism refuses to participate. Whence comes such a difference between the two parts of the separated Church? The participation of Orthodoxy in this movement does not all signify that it can renounce any portion whatever of its traditon or that it can accept a compromise or reconsideration. On the other hand, relations with heterodox confessions may aid the Orthodox Church to attain greater plenitude and breadth. Orthodoxy is present at such conferences to testify to the truth. These conferences are not councils, they are only preliminary assemblies, they are "conciliation." There are no reasons why Orthodoxy should avoid conferences. On the contrary, Christian love demands that the faith be testified to, that one be "all things to all men," as the Apostle said, "in order that by all means I might save some" (I Cor. 9:22). Orthodoxy is not separated from the rest of the Christian world by a wall of absolute power, the papacy, whose preliminary recognition is imposed. Since this obstacle does not exist for Orthodoxy, it can enter into relations, in all liberty and sincerity, with the whole Christian world, remaining always that which it is itself. The Orthodox Church does not put its hopes on human efforts and the missionary zeal of its members, but it hopes in the power of the Spirit of God, Who lives in the Church and Who is leading the peoples toward unity. This unity may be found only in Orthodoxy. The Christian peoples of the world are now seeking Orthodoxy, often without knowing it. And they will find it, for it is said: "Seek and ye shall find."

CHAPTER 18

CONCLUSION

At the present time, historic Orthodoxy is passing through a crisis. Its enemies see in this crisis death and destruction, but we Orthodox should see in it the beginning of a new era. This crisis is connected with the Russian revolution, and with the fall of the Russian Orthodox Empire. It may be compared in importance with the fall of Byzantium and the taking of Constantinople by the Turks, when the Christian world, and the Orthodox world especially, sustained a similar blow. We have perhaps witnessed the end of the Constantinian period in Church history. At this very hour, the Russian Church, the greatest among Orthodox Churches, lies beneath the yoke of the most terrible persecution history has ever seen. In the eyes of the unbelieving, its very existence is menaced. But to the eyes of those who believe, the Russian Church appears as chosen among all Christianity, that it may, after having passed through a trial by fire, testify in spirit, in truth, and in liberty. In this sense it is impossible not to see in the destinies of the Russian Church the fate of all Christianity, the conflict of the whole of the Christian Church with the hordes of the Anti-Christ. The exclusion of Russia from the life of the world makes impossible the reestablishment of economic and political life; in the same way, without the Russian Church, the most important questions of Christian unity cannot be decided. All Christians who now discover the need of facing a new future, are beginning to understand the world importance of the destinies of Orthodoxy.

Does that future exist for the Church? Yes, for Orthodoxy is not yet achieved, either in fact, or even in principle. Above Orthodoxy there is no other dome than the vault of heaven. The Orthodox Church has heard and believes the promise of Our Lord Jesus Christ about the Holy Spirit, the Comforter Who ''will declare the things to come.'' The Orthodox Church is now faced with new problems,

193

new perspectives, it contains not only the end but the creative way which leads to it. "Thy youth shall be renewed like that of the eagle" (Psalm 10:5). The spirit of God the Creator who lives in the Church calls to this renewal of which the Saviour has said: "It is without measure that the Lord bestows the Spirit."

This creative inspiration, to which is added religious inspiration, will bring in a new era of creative Christian life. A similar period in history is the "Middle Age," both in East and West. This gave way to the "Modern Ages," which in turn must lead to a "New Middle Ages," for which, consciously or not, the leading minds of Christianity have longed. That can come about only on one condition, the existence of liberty which cannot be renounced by humanity—humanity which is now become ripe for the plenitude of the life of the Church, with its gifts of grace. It is Orthodoxy, and Orthodoxy only, which is the manifest and the hidden truth of all Christian confessions, divided now, but called to reunite in one flock under One Pastor. May God grant it!

INDEX

NOTES

NOTES

NOTES

NOTES

NOTES

NOTES

NOTES

NOTES